SIX FEET DEEP

Burying Your Past with Forgiveness

Freely Forgive &
Live Freely!

Blessings,

[signature]

Rev. 12:11

My special thanks is extended to all of my immediate and biological family along with my friends and acquaintances for their encouragement and provision of information for my writing of this book. I especially express my thanks and appreciation to a Tulsa County District Judge, the Tulsa County Court Clerk's Office, Los Angeles County District Attorney's Office, Los Angeles County Court Clerk's Office, Los Angeles Archives Department, a U.S. Senator, the Salvation Army, Social Security Administration, U.S. Supreme Court for the State of Oklahoma, and U.S. Military Records Division for their assistance and provision of documentations, records, and information that I received.

SIX FEET DEEP

Burying Your Past with Forgiveness

B. Steve Young

A BOLD TRUTH Publication
Christian Literature & Artwork

Unless otherwise noted, all Scripture quotations are from the New King James Version of the Bible. Copyright 1979,1980, 1982, by Thomas Nelson Inc., Publishers. Used by permission.

Scripture quotations marked NLT are from the New Living Translation, copyright 1996, 2004, 2007 by the Tyndale House Foundation. Used by permission of Tyndale House Publishers, Inc., Carol Stream Illinois 60188.

All names of the persons mentioned in this book have been changed to preserve the privacy, maintain integrity, and protection for those who are innocent. Any similarity between individuals described in this book, either by name or character, known to the readers is purely and strictly coincidental.

SIX FEET DEEP
Burying Your Past In Forgiveness
© 2013 Doors of Compassion Ministries, Inc.

ISBN 13: 978-0-9915751-3-8

B. Steve Young
P.O. Box 974
Sapulpa, Oklahoma 74067

BOLD TRUTH PUBLISHING
Christian Literature & Artwork
606 West 41st, Ste. 4
Sand Springs, Oklahoma 74063
beirep@yahoo.com

Printed in the USA.

This book and its contents thereof may not be reproduced in any form, stored in a retrieval system, photocopied, recorded, or otherwise - without the prior written consent and permission of the author and publisher, as provided by the United States of America copyright law.

Cover Design: Aaron Jones ▪ *www.WildArtByAaron.com*

CONTENT

Foreword..*i*

Introduction..*iii*

Chapter 1
In the Beginning..1

Chapter 2
A Time to Rebuild...5

Chapter 3
Kidnapped..11

Chapter 4
Unity, Division & Growth..15

Chapter 5
Prunning...19

Chapter 6
More Prunning..27

Chapter 7
A Fresh Start..39

Chapter 8
Starting Over...45

Chapter 9
Incompatabilities..51

Chapter 10
Times of Hardship..59

Chapter 11
Starting Over Again..71

Chapter 12
Making Adjustments..79

Chapter 13
Fulfilling the Birthday Wish..85

Chapter 14
Reunion Plans..93

Chapter 15
Hidden in the Dirt..103

Chapter 16
Maturity..107

Chapter 17
Lies..111

Chapter 18
Instruction in Forgiveness..117

Chapter 19
Choices...125

Foreword

Forgiveness is a tough lesson any way you learn it. My friend Steve demonstrates forgiveness just by living and ministering every day of his life. The story that he tells here is so incredible that it reaches the level of disbelief…unless you know the truth of his character. You'll not only read some hard-to-fathom details of how life (and people) has treated him, but you'll also read about a faithful God who was working from the beginning on a plan that can't be denied.

I felt like I knew Steve well after traveling with him to prisons and ministering with him occasionally over several years. But I had never realized the trauma that he'd been forced to face early in life. As I read his story, I learned several new lessons about love and forgiveness from a man that I know walks in love, without having to justify any step he takes. He just loves God.

Steve's ministry to prisoners all across our state and the country demonstrates the compassion of a man who knows what it's like to be incarcerated. He doles out the forgiveness of his own experience to every prisoner he meets…in abundant doses. That ministry has proven itself day by day with more doors of opportunity opening regularly. There is a great need for that kind of compassion and ministry in our world, and Steve and Rita are out there doing what's needed wherever those doors open.

Blessings to all who read!
Roland J. Depew
Full Gospel Evangelistic Association
Representative to Victory Bible College

Introduction

Throughout our lives, we all experience situations where we become hurt or abused physically, mentally, emotionally, or a combination of all three. Some people encounter these hurts worse than others. It's how we handle these life's confrontations that determines our personal destiny and growth above the situations. Are we willing to forgive?

The issue of forgiveness is often one of the most difficult obstacles a person must face head on and overcome. Forgiveness doesn't excuse the behavior of another person, instead, your forgiveness prevents their behavior from destroying your heart and life.

I did not write this book just to be writing one or to become declared as an author. The Lord burned this message into my heart to share this subject with others to help them with the unhappiness through their unforgiveness they are struggling with. I'm thankful for my friends, family, and pastor who encouraged me to follow through with this writing.

I believe many will be set free and relationships restored from the bondage of unforgiveness as they read this book and obey the instruction from the Holy Spirit's prompting to them, just as it did for me.

Chapter 1
In the Beginning

It was the early morning hours of June 16, 1951. My life began almost like everyone else's, with the welcoming of newly proud parents and other family members. I was greeted with kisses, smiles, and coos from all around. It was the first day of a life full of hope and opportunity. Little did I or anyone else know of the hurdles and destiny of my life that was ahead of me, and the hurts and challenges that I would face. The fact is, none of us including you who are reading this know what our future holds ahead. Only God Himself knows that answer, as Scripture says.

Six months later tragedy struck our new happily made family, as my mother Carol was diagnosed with a tumor that was located within a section of her brain. The doctors saw it in the x-rays and suggested surgery. After several hours of surgery, the doctors were unable to locate the tumor. They decided to let her rest under sedation overnight and try again the following morning. But morning never came for my mother. In the middle of the night, she developed an aneurysm near the site of the tumor and it ruptured. My mother died at the young age of twenty and I, as an infant, had experienced my first loss. Though it was a first for me, it was something my mother and I shared: loss at an early age.

GOING BACK IN TIME

At five years old, my mother and her one year old brother, Glen, watched as their own mother, Ellen, become ill. Ellen contracted a virus and developed respiratory difficulties. She later died at the age of 27.

SIX FEET DEEP

Ellen's husband, Carl, was a prominent orthopedic surgeon in his community. He soon experienced the difficulties that most single parents face: how to raise children and have a successful career. Carl was more fortunate than some, as he had four sisters. One of his sisters, Luby, was divorced, so she moved in with him to help with the daily house chores and care for the children. Grandpa Carl's other three sisters also all pitched in from time to time to offer their assistance when needed.

YEARS GONE BY

In the fall of 1948 at the age of seventeen and fresh out of high school, Carol met a handsome young man named Perry, who had just completed serving with the Marine Corps. It was described as love at first sight and a match made from heaven.

Within just a few months they eloped to Yuma, Arizona and got married. Their initial plan was to keep it a secret, but they had eloped with another couple. The other newlywed bride told her mother, and her mother told Carl.

In the meantime Perry had told his mother Regina, because he like his sister Brenda, was always close and able to confide in their mother. Regina wasn't exactly keen on the idea of what Perry and Carol had just done but felt, "Ok, what's done is done, now let's make the best of the situation." She liked Carol very much but felt that she and Perry were both too young and that they hadn't known each other very long to be getting married so soon.

Grandpa Carl was furious over the news of the marriage and called Regina to talk about it. It was with his intent that he suggested that Carol was to never see Perry again, and wanted Regina to enforce Perry to do the same. She disagreed with Carl, feeling that the young couple should both continue to live in their own homes and let time pass in allowing the to get to know each other better. She then expressed that

In the Beginning

with his attempt to keep them apart would only drive them closer toward each other.

Still enraged over the situation, Carl whisked Carol off to Lake Tahoe where she stayed with another one of Carl's sisters for a few weeks, claimed a Nevada residency, and got an annulment of the marriage filed. At that time Nevada required a residency period of six weeks for such actions to be filed.

After returning to their home in Glendale and over the course of the next few months Carol would still see Perry, but not with the knowledge or permission of her father. Instead, she pretended to be dating another young man. Then when that young man came to pick her up, he immediately took her to where Perry was.

Then one weekend, and on the day of her eighteenth birthday, a well made out plan came to pass. Perry drove up to the front of Carol's house, she walked out with her luggage in hand, got in Perry's car, and they rode off together into the sunset. Within a few days later they again became married.

TWO EVENTFUL YEARS

A year and a half year later, the year 1951 could have very well been described or known as the good, the bad, and the ugly.

"The good" had two parts with the first being with the celebration of my birth. It was done so a little later that initially planned, as my due date of arrival was originally set to be closer to Carol's birthday in May. Better a little late than never!

The second part of "the good" was from the gift that Perry & Carol received from Silver, another one of Carl's other sisters. As a wedding gift she gave them the money required for the down payment to buy the home they liked in Manhattan Beach.

Here it was, the beginning of October, a young happily married couple with their four month old son, and now looking forward to spending Christmas in their first new home as a family. What could possibly ever go wrong?

A month and a half later "the bad" happened, causing the shattering of dreams and the lives left behind with the death of my mother.

"The ugly" in uncertainty of the time or place, Carl became reacquainted with a younger single woman named Janet. She was a patient of Carl's earlier in her life when she was quite young. When she became an adult she began a career as a secretary with the city attorney's office. Now at the age of 28 and Carl's age of 60, they went to Las Vegas in March 1952 and became married. The reception they received upon their return home was not the usual of happiness and welcoming. Instead it was more like fireworks among the family, particularly with Luby and her sisters, as they were in no offering their condolences with this relationship mainly because of the age differences.

NOTES:

Chapter 2
A Time to Rebuild

After the loss of my mother, my father faced the same challenges that my grandfather Carl encountered in the passing of his wife. One major difference though was that my father didn't have a professional career background and therefore struggled maintaining employment and raising me at the same time.

Although my father occasionally drank, it didn't become a more frequent part of his life until after mother's death. He didn't show very much responsibility about taking care of me, and the combination of both of these would later come back and plague him in a legal battle.

Another thing that he had in common with my grandfather was that he had his sister to fall back on for support, who also was available and willing to help, as well as their mother. Brenda and her husband Mack were close to celebrating their fourth wedding anniversary when the loss of my mother occurred, as well as the birth of their first child Patty, who was born the week following.

Even with the beginning of the new addition to their own and now growing family, they still found room and made it possible for me to spend a lot of my time to be under their nurturing care in their home. There were numerous times where I would spend anywhere from one day to weeks or months with them as my father was either working, out of town, or going where ever and doing what ever.

SIX FEET DEEP

A TIME FOR CORRECTION

As I began to grow and develop physically, I was diagnosed with a severe case of Genu Valgum, commonly known as "knock knees."

Grandpa Carl invented a brace device along with the use of corrective shoes to correct this disability. I was chosen, so-to-speak, to be the one who would test his products. As I grew brace adjustments and new sizes were required.

A TIME FOR NEW CUSTODY

I'm not sure of the names of or how my father made the acquaintances with an older couple, but sometime in 1956 through the late spring / early summer of 1957 I lived with this couple while attending kindergarten.

Soon after school was out I remember Janet came by informing the older couple and me that grandpa Carl wanted me to move into his home and live with him and Janet. Supposedly at some time prior to this, she had been sent out by grandpa Carl to check on my well being, and in doing so she found me eating out of a trash can. After her finding this discovery, he told her to go get me and bring me to their home.

I question this as I do remember living with this couple and this is not one of the memories I have from doing so. They always seemed to show acts of kindness, if not love, towards me as well as keeping me well nourished, clothed, and provided for.

Apparently it was disturbing to grandpa that I was being bounced around from different places and homes and not having a solid family and home upbringing. With this in mind, along with the facts that my father hadn't shown very much responsibility about taking care of me and a developing drinking problem, my grandfather decided to seek the custody and with later intentions of adopting me.

A Time to Rebuild

On June 3rd, a petition for a temporary appointment of guardianship was filed. Then on July 26th the court granted temporary custody of me to grandpa Carl, along with a continued date set for January 6, 1958.

A TIME OF FEW MEMORIES

The next several months began with new adjustments, adventures, school, and holidays. My memory of moving into my grandfather's house is somewhat limited, yet those memories remain strong and alive. I recall that it was a rather large home with a big front porch, and a line of avocado trees on one side that separated it from the house next door. In the back yard was a tennis court where I occasionally rode my bicycle and wagon. Between the tennis court and the house was a couple of pomegranate bushes. Being that little normal and curious all-American boy (like the cartoon character that lived next door to Mr. Wilson) that I was, the temptation to pick and bite into one of those pinkish red and juicy balls seemed to get to the best of me several times. And each time that it did, I always seemed to have on a different clean T-shirt, meaning that I began to have a collection of permanently stained shirts, of which I blamed the cause of that on to the little boy who lived next door.

The weather in during the summer in Glendale was at times hot during the day and cooler temperatures at night. There was a screened enclosed porch area on one side of the house where I occasionally slept at night, as I liked the cool air and light breezes that might blow through.

I've been told later, that I used to have nightmares when I first moved in with grandpa Carl and Janet. I have no idea if this is true or not as I do not recollect any of those times, and this is one of those things I question.

I only have two vivid memories of events that I spent with grandpa Carl. To some these may seem only trivial, but to me it's all I have and they're equally as important.

SIX FEET DEEP

The first was on one of the first mornings after I moved in with him. We were about to have breakfast, and he pulled out some type of small white electric kitchen appliance. He then took some fresh oranges, cut them in half, and pressed the open cut side of the orange onto the appliance, which in turn created fresh squeezed orange juice. We know it today as "juicer" or fruit juice making machine, but I had never seen anything like this before and I was very intrigued with it.

The second was the road trip that he and Janet took me on to go see the beauty of the National Redwood Forest. The height of those of trees were absolutely amazing to me. I can also recall the numerous semis carrying logs that we passed on the highway along the way. The grand finale of that trip of course, was our driving through the cut out hole in one of those trees at the entrance of the forest park.

The beginning of school began shortly after that trip and I started in the first grade. I can't recall seeing very much of grandpa Carl from then on. Time seemed to pass rather quickly as the next thing I remember was it was now Halloween. I either hit a bumper crop or else the local neighbors were very generous with the amount of candy and treats that they passed out, as I had two large bags full of treats.

Thanksgiving must have came and left without me because I don't have any recollection or memory of any events of this holiday that took place.

ANOTHER TIME OF LOSS

December was quickly upon us and the house had a few decorations to remind us that Christmas would soon be here. Then a couple of events occurred. The first was with the visit of some people that I had never met before. Their names were Greg and Aubrey, who were Janet's stepfather and mother, and had come from Oklahoma.

The second event was the cause and reason for Greg and Aubrey's

A Time to Rebuild

visit. It wasn't for the celebration of the Christmas holiday, instead it was due to the death of grandpa Carl.

The reason I didn't see him as very much earlier was because he had become ill and had to be hospitalized. He developed a disease known as sarcoidosis. It's cause is unknown but is a disease that can effect any organ. It's a disease in which abnormal collections of inflammatory cells form as nodules (benign cysts), which can cause an infection in the lungs and lead to respiratory failure, as it did to him on December 14th.

NOTES:

NOTES:

Chapter 3
Kidnapped

As we began the new year with the recent holidays and death of my grandfather behind us, the fate of my future was now in the hands of Janet. With the January 6th court date just a few days away, Janet filed a petition for appointment of guardianship on the January 3rd. As a result of that filing the case was continued with a court hearing set for March 19th.

Soon after her filing of that petition and in the middle of the night or very early in the morning (either way it was still dark outside), I remember Janet waking me up and the two of us along with her Bedlington Terrior went outside, got in the car, and went for a short drive. We arrived at someone's home and then transferred all of our belongings from the car we were in into another car. Within a short time we got into this other car and went for one very long trip.

After arriving to our apparent final destination, we pulled into the driveway of a small home. Greeting us at the front door was...Aubrey and Greg. Quite obvious we were now in Oklahoma. I didn't know or come to realize until later that my time of living and seeing my family in California was over.

HANG OUT OR HIDE OUT?

Janet began making a few short return trips to California leaving me behind to stay with Greg and Aubrey. My living with them reminded me a little like being with the older couple that I lived with in California. Aubrey seemed to enjoy entertaining me with games and activities, as well as with making me home made cookies and desserts. She fit the typical description of a "grandma", where grandchildren could do no wrong, and spoil the grandchild and then send him home. Greg worked for a large aerospace company, and when at home he enjoyed spending most of his evenings and weekends watching television - particularly sports, so I didn't spend very much time with him.

MAKING FRIENDS

I soon became acquainted with a family who were close friends of Greg and Aubrey, and who also shared some things in common. Aubrey was very active with a fraternal organization as was their friend Doris. Greg was also an active member of this organization, although their friend Duane wasn't, because he couldn't ever get accepted and voted in. It was called or known as being "black balled". However, Duane also worked at the same aerospace company where Greg worked, as a systems engineer.

Duane and Doris had two children, Dan (8), and his younger sister Bonita (5) who I got to spent a lot of time and play with. Janet continued to make trips to California allowing me to spend the range of a few days to a week at a time at their home. One of our favorite places to play was in a loft area in the garage where Dan kept his electric train set and other toys. A bond in our relationship began among us, as Dan and Bonita became more like a brother and sister to me, and Doris used to always refer to me as "one of her own".

RULES OF THE HOUSE

I can't recall what I did that was so horrible to require discipline, but I do remember the punishment, and as Janet would state it, "to teach me a lesson".

Kidnapped

She used a piece of small rope or twine tie my hands together behind my back, had me to sit on the toilet with the lid down, closed and locked the bathroom door. After a while of sitting in there and leaning my back against the wall, I started to swing my legs a little and bouncing my feet off the floor. I did that to help entertain myself as well as pass the time. Apparently I wasn't supposed to do that either, because she came in, tied my ankles together and added more time to the length of time I was to stay in there. Still determined to find a way of keeping myself occupied throughout this ordeal (again like the cartoon character little boy who lived next door to Mr. Wilson) I started loosening the knot of the rope that was binding my hands together. After a while I became successful in my efforts. I soon heard Janet coming so I started trying to slip my hands back into the loops of the rope as she began unlocking the bathroom door. She discovered what I had done, so she re-tied my hands together even tighter and added one more hour to my time in the bathroom. Do you suppose I broke another house rule? I didn't attempt to make any further rope adjustments as I just sat that final hour out. When the time was up, Janet untied and removed the rope/twine which left deep and red imprints in my wrists from being bound so tight.

A LEGAL MATTER

It was now the beginning of summer as Greg and Aubrey began a remodeling project by adding a den to the back of their house. I'm only making mention of this for now, as I will make reference to it later in the next chapter.

When fall arrived it began with my enrollment into the second grade. Although we didn't have any classes together because of the difference of our ages and grade levels, I soon learned that Dan and Bonita also attended this same school. We did however occasionally get to see each other in the hallways, playground, and cafeteria.

Within several weeks of this new school year, there was one

particular day that I would not attend. Instead, Janet and Aubrey took me to a place where once again I would briefly see the faces of new strangers. The one thing that vividly remains in my memory of this event is that we were sitting in a room (office) and a man asked me a questions that were uttered so fast that I didn't understand anything that he was asking. Even today I have no idea what the questions were. As I look over toward Aubrey, I saw her smiling big and she along with Janet were nodding their heads up and down as to coach or coerce me into doing the same. So I followed along I nodded my head up and down and later said, "Yes". It wasn't until a few short years later that I learned after having it explained to me what this incident consisted of…I had become adopted.

HOLIDAY SEASON

I may not have remembered anything about the Thanksgiving holiday from the previous year while in California, but I remember this one. Aubrey was very gifted in knowing how to cook. I truly believe she could have made boiled water taste good. I certainly and honestly can say that Janet never learned any traits from her mother in cooking, as later in this book I'll provide some examples from her menu There's an old saying "they cooked for an army" when in reference to a person who cooked a large amount of food, and Aubrey definitely fulfilled that description. I had never seen so much food in my entire life…all seven years of it.

Christmas quickly arrived afterward with its splendor of decorations. Aubrey's tree wasn't a big one, yet very fascinating to me. Instead of the typical green with either the thick fern or long thin pine needles, this tree was shiny and silver. Then and almost like magic the tree would change colors from its original silver to red, green, yellow, and blue. I soon came to learn that a light on the floor with a rotating disk with these colored sections caused these color changes. In addition to the colors of decorations and lights of course was the celebration with all of the presents and food.

Chapter 4
Unity, Division & Growth

Reflecting back momentarily to the previous summer Greg and Aubrey began their remodeling project. I'm not sure how or where they initially met, but they hired a brick mason to set the cinder blocks used for the outside walls of the den that was being added on to the back of the house.

During the construction process of this remodeling project, a romance developed between Janet and the brick mason named Earl. I can only presume that the reasons I was unaware of this relationship at the time is because of the numerous times that I had spent part of the summer staying at Duane & Doris' home, and possibly with the number of Janet's travels to California. Either one or both, I was used to not seeing her very often.

Now returning to the beginning of a new year, Janet and Earl advanced their relationship to another level. On the weekend of January 11th, they went to a small town southeast of Tulsa and united in marriage. Upon their return Janet and I moved into Earl's home, joining him and his daughter Louise.

I immediately transferred and began attending another school to complete the second grade as this move placed me in another school district. Louise was a few years older than me, and we occasionally walked to school together when the weather allowed, just as we did in the summer months to a public swimming pool that was near the school.

SIX FEET DEEP

With my estimation, during the latter part of the summer, Janet (who was now approximately pregnant) and I moved out of Earl's home and back into Greg and Aubrey's home. At the time I didn't understand or know the reason behind this move, although I was told that on multiple occasions Earl pawned some of Janet's personal belongings in order to have extra money to support his drinking habit. I have since learned of some additional information regarding their relationship and will reveal it later in the truth vs. fiction section of this book.

WEATHERED

I soon started school for the third grade and returned to the elementary school where I had attended during portions of the first and second grades, and once again occasionally saw Dan and Bonita.

There was a portion of the fall season where it rained for several days, and I was bought some outer rain wear. It was a heavy yellow plastic coat with a cloth type lining and it came with a matching hood that covered my head that snapped under my chin, which had an opening in the front just big enough to let my face be seen. I hated it!

The street just around the corner was part of my route in walking to school, and it had a lot of pot holes. I can remember that on one of those rainy mornings I was told to wear the rain coat and hood, but I didn't really want to. But regardless of my objections, I ended up wearing it. You might could say that I had assistance and persuasion in putting it on.

As I walked around the corner, I noticed that the pot holes were full of water. Being the typical and all-american boy that I was, I took off my rain coat, laid it on top of one of the pot holes full of water, got down on my back, and rolled around on my rain coat just like a dog does rolling around on its back. I think maybe that I was just testing out to see how water proof the coat was. It was quite fun as I did this until - I looked up toward the sky, and there stood a woman with her hands on both hips and staring down at me. It was Janet. She grabbed me by the arm and in a hurried pace almost dragged me home, had me to change into some clean dry clothes, and then drove me to school. After I got home later from school, I got a whipping with the use of a tree switch like I had never had before, that left red and bleeding whelps on both legs.

NEW ARRIVALS

Within a few weeks later and when school let out, I was met by another family friend named Emma. She and her husband William lived a couple of blocks away from Greg and Aubrey's house, and I passed it in route to school. They too had a couple of children that were both adopted, and I believe William may have also worked at the same aerospace company that Greg and Duane worked at.

The reason Emma met and picked me up at school and taken to her home is because Janet was taken to the hospital by Aubrey earlier in the day. Later when evening approached Janet gave birth to twin boys - Byron and Brett. It was later declared that this was the best present she had ever received, as this same day was her birthday.

Almost immediately I was no longer the center of attention as due to the birth of Byron and Brett. I really never noticed that because I entertained myself with my toy cars and making believe that I was a cowboy with the western characters that I watched on television. This particularly true around the Christmas holiday.

NOTES:

Chapter 5
Prunning

The new year of 1960 began as one of a pruning process. Just as a gardener prunes and trims a tree or bush by cutting away some of its branches and limbs for later growth, they must first reduce its present condition of unwanted portions. In her own selective way, Janet pruned the unwanted portions (lives) within her own family. In doing so, she filed for divorce shortly after the birth of Byron and Brett. On January 28th the divorce between her and Earl became official and in effect.

Janet reverted back to carrying "Young" as her last name and changed it to that for Byron and Brett as well. Starting early she raised them with the belief that my grandpa Carl was their father therefore making them and me brothers.

The following day Janet began a new growth process with the purchase of a house in the same hundred block as Greg & Aubrey but one block over. Over the next few months Greg spent his weekends helping Janet with wallpapering and painting of the inside and outside of the house in preparation for us to move into.

NO TALKING

I was reminded on multiple occasions and times by Janet "children are to be seen and not heard", and that rule was apparently true especially at church. About a mile from Greg and Aubrey's house is was a Christian church that Aubrey and Janet attended occasionally, as well as where Greg would take and drop me off every Sunday morning for Sunday school. On the Sunday's that Aubrey or Janet attended, I would usually meet up with one or both of them after Sunday school and sit with them during the morning worship service. There was one particular Sunday that they were running late as I didn't see either one of them after the service began, so I sat toward the front with some other children my age as I had at previous times before. Being children we probably paid more attention to playing connect the dots, tic-tac-toe, etc, instead of listening to the minister. About midway through the service Janet entered the isle where I was sitting in and sat down between the other children and me. I didn't realize it at the time but I had broken another house rule as after we got home she told Greg that I had been talking and disruptive during the church service. He grabbed the leather strap which was about an inch wide and a quarter-inch thick that was used occasionally to walk their boxer, took me outside into the backyard, grabbed my left wrist, and had me running in circles and jumping due to the whipping he gave me.

Another time of talking when I wasn't supposed to resulted in Janet taking me into the bathroom, then soaking a wash cloth with warm water and bar soap, and then cramming it into my mouth until I almost gagged.

MORE HOUSE RULES

In my days of attending the third grade, the lunches served in the cafeteria were more nourishing than what they are today. In addition they were more pleasing to the eye than the usual cheese, potted meat, or lunchmeat sandwiches that I took to school for lunch. I met up with Dan one day as he was close to finishing his lunch and was about to begin eating his dessert. I sat down beside him, opened up my lunch pail, and just stared at what I was about to partake of. Then I looked over at the plate that Dan had just eaten from and the tempting dessert that he was about to devour, and quickly decided that his meal was much more better than what I was about to eat. I excused myself, walked over to the trash can, dumped out all the contents from my lunch pail, grabbed a tray, went down the line picking out all of the food items that I wanted, and rejoined Dan at the table where he was still sitting. I didn't know it at the time these meals required either a meal ticket or money and had to be paid for. I say this because I didn't ever see very many, if any, of the other students paying out any money, and must have thought the food was free, as I did this quite frequently. It got to the point that this was working so well that I never really looked at what inside my lunch pail and all the contents automatically met Mr. Trash Can.

I must have been set up because one day after I came home from school, I was questioned by Janet and Aubrey about my lunch...how did I like it, what did I have, and did I like the extra surprise that was in it? I failed by providing the wrong answers. Apparently they had received a telephone call from the school regarding the lunches that I had become accustomed to having daily and on a regular basis. Along with the whipping I received after Greg got home, for punishment Janet would pick me up at my scheduled lunch time, take me home, had me to scoop up the dog poop in the backyard, and then again after school for several days. And now to think that people have made businesses doing this. I created a business as a pooper scooper and didn't know it.

BROKEN TRUSTS

One evening Greg and I were home alone while Aubrey and Janet were away for a few hours, possibly attending one of the fraternity meetings. We were in the den watching television when Greg got up from the sofa that he usually sprawled out on, closed and locked the entrance door, went into one of the closets, pulled out some books and magazines, and began showing them to me. They contained pictures of women that were either naked or wearing swimsuits. I wasn't exactly comfortable about this, but then again I had never experienced this before either. Then after a little later he had me to perform a sexual act for his satisfaction.

SIX FEET DEEP

The next morning I told Janet what had occurred. She apparently put it aside because I never heard anymore about it from her, but got in trouble later with Greg for my telling her what he had me to do.

INCORRIGIBLE OUTCAST

After the birth of Byron and Brett it seemed that maybe I wasn't really wanted anymore. It wasn't an issue of me becoming jealous from the twins receiving more attention than me, as newborns do require more attention and care. However, I began sensing things had changed and that I was in the way but couldn't explain it to anyone.

There was a medical center for children located in the south part of Tulsa that housed physical and mentally handicapped children that were also under privileged, who required either physical or psychological assistance. They apparently also offered and received walk in patients for psychological counseling because Janet scheduled multiple appointments for me to be seen by a psychologist. In her terms, I was an incorrigible child because I heard her describe me as this multiple times. In my terms, I don't think she could or knew how to handle a typical all-American boy who: 1) has started off life with many struggles and hurts; 2) needed to be shown love in its full meaning vs. continued and added hurts; and 3) wouldn't fit within her set mold.

These counseling sessions started out with one or two times a month for a few hours at a time until...school was out for the summer...and I became a resident at that medical center. I really didn't mind though because it wasn't too bad of a place to stay. There were other children to play with, Saturday nights were movie and popcorn nights, and all of us children were shown attention in a loving way.

The counseling sessions continued twice a week. Even to this day I never understood the reason or purpose behind them or what they were to accomplish, as most of the time they consisted of this psychologist

Prunning

taking me out to a nearby ice cream parlor for a treat, watching him shoot at a skeet practice range, or whatever mood he was for. I can only recall us having any serious conversations a couple of times and can't even remember what these conversations consisted of.

At the end of the summer I was told that I would be leaving from there in a few days. Naturally I thought that I would be returning to what was to be considered "home" at Janet's. Instead, on the day that I left the medical center the counselor took me to the Tulsa Boys Home where I would live. My first few days there was spent in a dorm where I had a room to myself as there weren't any other boys in the building. I was then moved over to another dorm that had other boys that were close to my age and into a room where I would share with two other roommates.

I adjusted pretty well and quickly adapted to this habitat and had free reign to move around. On weekdays I'd walk to school which was approximately six blocks away. On Saturdays we were allowed to walk to the downtown area to any of the theaters to watch a movie, and on Sundays we would walk to a church of our choice. Occasionally for those who had and wanted to spend time with their parents, we could be checked out for the weekends. I can only remember of two or three times that Janet checked me out during the nine months that I lived there. One of those times I didn't want to go, and I told her when she came to pick me up that I had gotten "campused". She found out this wasn't true so she went ahead and checked me out for the weekend and then grounded me.

At the end of the nine months that I lived at the boys' home, the school year had just completed, and it was now the beginning of summer. I don't recall any events during the summer that occurred other than I got to reunite with Dan and Bonita. However, toward the end of summer Janet told me to mow the back yard. While mowing I noticed a patch of weeds so I mowed over them as well. I learned later that this patch was not weeds at all...it was a small strawberry patch.

SIX FEET DEEP

Although I didn't know this, I still got in trouble. As like many times of occurrence of the past as well as the years ahead, she slapped me and spit in my face. Something else also occurred at this particular time that had not occurred in the past...I stood up for myself. In the middle of my getting into trouble for mowing over the strawberry plants, Janet called me a son-of-a-b_ _ _ h. I retaliated by telling her that, "I was not a son-of-a-b_ _ _h, my mother was NOT a b_ _ _h, she never even knew my mother, and that I never wanted hear her call my mother that name again."

When fall arrived and it was time to start school again, Janet decided to enroll me into the Catholic school that was one block over and behind our house instead of my returning to elementary school where I had attended before. I believe her reasoning behind this decision is because it goes back to the days when she was young and raised by her grandmother who sent Janet to a Catholic school. Additionally I believed Janet was convinced and even made statements that the Catholic school would provide me a better education as well as being a more disciplined school that what the public schools would provide.

The discipline measures and religious beliefs they offered did not settle or agree with me very well. There were two incidents in particular that occurred and still remain in my memories. The first was during a particular mass service that we were required to attend during the middle of the morning. Walking into the sanctuary area, dipping my finger in "Holy Water" and doing the cross symbol was not a problem to me. However, on this particular mass something happened that bothered me. A high priest, bishop, or whatever position he held came an outside guest. Our class entered into the sanctuary, completed the cross symbol with the "Holy Water", knelt at the end of the isle, and did the cross symbol again as usual. Before entering the isle to sit, on this occassion we were expected to kiss a ring that this guest wore on one of his fingers as he extended his hand out. As I entered the pew to where I would be kneeling and sitting, this special guest quietly cleared

Prunning

his throat and grabbed my arm. He looked me straight in the eye, and without saying anything, he used his eyes as a jester in looking down to the ring. I refused to kiss the ring and it offended him. This apparently created a problem as Janet was later called, and I was disciplined for being "disrespectful." I'm not trying to be disrespectful, but I didn't kiss a ring then, and I won't kiss anyone's ring today either. I do not see any where in Scripture that Jesus or His disciples had this practice.

The second incident occurred a few weeks later when I was denied twice after asking to be excused to go use the restroom. After my third time of asking, I was sent to the back of the classroom and into an area where we hung our coats because I was "disrupting the class". The cloak room area had a wall that divided it from the classroom, and therefore no one could see me, or me them. I was in a real dilemma as I really had to "go" bad! I ended up relieving myself there in the coat room. This of course got me in trouble with the school and with Janet. After I got home, I got another one of those beatings of my life and was sent to live with Greg and Aubrey.

NOTES:

NOTES:

Chapter 6
More Prunning

Within a few weeks before my completion of the fifth grade at the Catholic school, Janet arranged for me to become a "Ward of the Court". Shortly after the school year was finished I was taken to a boys ranch in Edmond, Oklahoma. Named the Baptist Boys Ranch Town, is sponsored by the Oklahoma Baptist Association as well as then by various Baptist churches across the state. Within those various churches were families who would each sponsor one boy. Throughout the year these sponsoring churches and families contributed to a specific fund that would help cover the costs for our clothing, special needs, and Christmas gifts. The first week or two of July was known as "sponsor's week" as when each boy was placed on a bus line, sent to the town where the sponsoring church and family were located, and he would stay with that sponsoring family for one week.

Every one of the boys who lived there experienced issues that challenged them as well as their parents, foster-parents, or guardians. Boys come to this campus for various reasons: too much conflict with families at home, DHS is involved with the case and requests placement at the ranch, those who exhibits too many behavioral problems and the parents or guardian needs or requests help, boys that are neglected and abused, or abandoned by their families and have no place to live. I believe the two reasons I was sent there were because: Janet no longer knew how or wanted to handle a typical all-American curious boy, and I believe this was mainly because of the birth of her own new twins. I was the adopted child and not her natural born child. That made a difference, and now I was in the way.

SIX FEET DEEP

When I arrived at "the ranch" I was the only boy on campus because all the other residents had just left a few days previously to start into "sponsor week". Therefore I spent my first week there wandering around and scouting out portions of the approximate 150 acres that it rested on. There were three cottages that housed all the boys, and each were broken down into the three school aged groups: elementary, junior high, and high school. Each cottage had their own set of house parents and a house cook. To the South and east of the cottages and campus superintendent's office and living quarters, was a winding sandy dirt road that led to where the chicken houses and a pond were.

INITIATIONS

At the end of my first week the campus and cottage rooms began to fill up as the boys were arriving from their return trip. It was the custom that within the first few weeks after the arrival of a newcomer, he would start experiencing initiations that are performed by the other resident boys. The reasoning behind these was to see how strong or weak the newcomer is. Not so much in physical strength but rather in emotional strength and weakness, plus to determine whether he will become a "snitch" or a "rat" or not.

I was no exception for these initiations. They began like small pranks, mainly to just get a good laugh or two. My first was when I was told by my two other roommates that since I was the last to bed one night, that I had to go down the hall and turn out the lights. I marched down the hallway without any incident, however, just as I got to the end of the hallway and reached out to turn off the lights, there stood our house mother. That wasn't so much the problem, except…I'm standing there in my underwear! She politely explained to me that she was the one who turns out the lights…each and every night. Totally red-faced with embarrassment I walked back down the hallway in returning to my room, and I could hear all the other boys giggling from within their rooms. After I returned to my room she turned out the lights…but

More Prunning

then I had difficulty getting into my bed and under the covers. Trying to be quiet as so that she wouldn't hear the commotion, I discovered that I had been short sheeted.

The next morning in the chow hall during breakfast, I reached out for the salt shaker to lightly sprinkle some salt on my scrambled eggs. As I turned the salt shaker upside down in the process of giving it a good shake...the metal cap of the shaker landed on top of my eggs...along with the entire contents of the salt shaker. One of the rules that we had to abide by was that we could eat all we wanted, but...we had to eat all the food that was on our plates. I was able to scrape off a large portion of the heap of salt, and managed to eat the scrambled eggs underneath.

The last prank type of initiation came on a Sunday morning as we began getting ready for church. While I had been in the shower, a couple of the other boys had sabotaged my clothes with a hand made smoke bomb. This consisted of using a clicking action ball point pen, a bobby pin, and a small wooden match. To make this work, the pen is unscrewed and the ink filler cartridge is removed. The hole at the tip of the pen had to be enlarged a little. Leaving the spring in the bottom half of the pen barrel, the bobby pin is fed through the spring, then the enlarged hole, and then flanged and folded out. The wooden match stick is inserted into the bottom barrel portion of the pen with the match head facing downward. The top portion of the pen is then screwed back onto the bottom barrel. The pen is then placed into the inside pocket of the suit coat or sports jacket with the pocket clip that is located on the top portion of the pen. Pulling down on the flanged and folded out part of the bobby pin and releasing it because it is now spring loaded, causes the head of the bobby pin to strike against the head of the match head. Since this ignition occurs inside the pen barrel, there isn't an open flame. Instead it creates a very foul odor from the smoke that it produces. Nevertheless, I wore that smelly suit as it was the only one I had, and no one would sit next to me either on the bus or even in church for that matter.

SIX FEET DEEP

The final initiation came a week or two later and was one that was not classified as either being a prank or funny. Three of the boys from my cottage wanted to give me a full tour of the ranch. We left the area in the front where the cottages were located, and started down the sandy dirt road that led to where the chicken houses and pond were. One of the boys opened a large door to the chicken house to show me the hundreds of caged chickens that were kept inside. As we stepped inside, three other boys from the high school cottage jumped and tackled me, and the next thing I knew I was flat on my back. Trying to get up and free from them was useless. Then appearing over me was a seventh boy, who had in one of his gloved hands a handful of fresh chicken manure that he had just grabbed from underneath one of the cages, and crammed it onto my face and into my mouth, forcing me to swallow it.

LIFE ON THE RANCH: HOUSE RULES

Like anywhere else there are always rules and regulations to live by, and "the ranch" didn't have any exceptions. Our days usually began around 5:30 a.m. and we were expected to quickly make our beds, shower, get dressed, eat breakfast, and either get on the bus to go to school or begin our daily assigned chores. During the summer, as it was in the case when I arrived there, the chores were assigned and divided out consisted of gardening, raising chickens and cleaning the chicken houses, mowing, baling hay, and feeding livestock. Our ages were not a factor in any of the chores that were assigned to us.

During the fall season there were chores of cleaning of the chicken houses, clearing of brush, chopping wood, and feeding livestock.

Our winter season chores included cleaning of the chicken houses as well as slaughtering of chickens, plucking feathers, cutting up of chickens for packing and freezing. Lunch time during this part of the year wasn't exactly the most desirable, because after returning to our cottage and getting cleaned up, our house cook always seemed to place

More Prunning

before us on the tables...fried chicken!

When spring arrived new baby chicks were either hatched by existing hens or bought for the new season. Our chores consisted of the feeding and raising of the new chicks and cleaning of the chicken houses. You might detect some consistency in one of these assigned chores.

Throughout the year there were times that our assigned chores wouldn't involve being outside of our cottages. This was because they were assigned to be performed inside such as: sweeping, mopping, waxing and buffing of the floors. If you really wanted to see a wild sight and enjoy a good laugh, watching a newcomer operate the buffing machine would do just that. Knowing when and how to lift up slightly on the handle to make the buffer go right and lightly pushing down on the handle to allow it to go left was an art. If you didn't, the machine would buck and take you along with it. There was also kitchen duty where one week a boy would clean off the tables in the dining area, one boy would wash the dishes, and a third boy would dry the dishes and put them up, in which all of these chores were individually assigned and then rotated at the end of the week for a week long assignment.

We also had to learn how to do our own laundry, as well as iron our own clothes. This meant that we sometimes had to learn the hard way that if the iron was set too hot some of our clothing came out with a melted or scorched look, or worse yet, a burnt area with the shape of the bottom of the iron on the clothes.

PRIVILEGES

After lunch on Saturdays we were allowed to board the campus bus and taken into town to a matinee theater where our admission cost to see a movie was twenty-five cents. For those who had girlfriends from school or church, this was also a time and place to meet up with them.

SIX FEET DEEP

On Sunday mornings we boarded the bus and were taken to the First Baptist Church for Sunday School and the morning worship service, as well as returning there later for the Sunday evening service.

Visitation by family members were usually allowed to occur for a few hours every other Sunday afternoon from 2:00 - 5:00. Depending upon our personal conduct regulated the type of visitation privileges that could or could not be allowed. For example, sometimes the family visitors could take their boy off-campus during that three hour period… if he didn't have any demerits against him. If there were only a small amount of demerits, the boy may be allowed to have visitation, but on-campus only. There were always cases where some of the boys were classified as "campused", because of too many demerits and therefore not allowed to have visitations. These merits and demerits were based on how successful or unsuccessful the boys' chores were completed, and or if they got into any trouble or fights during the week.

Then there were those who never got visitations because their family either never came to visit, or they didn't have any family to come see them. Off hand, I can only recall three times that Janet came to visit me, and if my memory serves me correctly I believe Aubrey joined along on the either the first or second visit. The third visit will be one that I discuss a little later in this chapter.

Along with watching some of the other boys have visitors while I didn't, the same held true for those who occasionally received mail and or packages. For most of the two years that I lived on the ranch, I can count on one hand the number of letters that I received. The one letter that really sticks out in my mind was the one I received within the first few months of my being there, and it was from either Janet or Aubrey telling me of the wonderful vacation they were having along with the twins in either California or Oregon. Apart from that letter, I may have received another one or two, but I do not remember any more than that. Instead my memory recalls more of the times that I didn't, such as when my birthday or Christmas times arrived and I didn't receive any cards or letters for those occasions, and watched those who did during their time of celebration. Even as I write this, I think about other kids even today in homes like this who never get the cards on special occassions that many kids get, wondering if anyone cares that they exist. I pray that in reading this book, that hearts are touched to consider some children's home out there that possibly might need Christians to reach out and let those kids know they are valuable to God.

RESTRICTIONS

Along with the rules and daily chores that we had to abide by, there were also restrictions that carried disciplinary actions. There was an open perimeter boundary of the ranch, which meant it wasn't surrounded by fences and barbed wire, but we were expected to remain within the perimeter of that property. In other words, if anyone ran away...and some did, the local law enforcement agencies would be notified...and they were. Once caught, instead of being returned to the ranch, the runaways were usually placed in a state detention center, where the perimeters were fenced and guarded, much like a prison.

Fighting was a forbidden rule along with no cussing, stealing, or smoking but they all occurred and all of these violations were usually and eventually caught. It was at times like these when privileges for going into town on Saturdays to go to the movies or Sunday visitations were taken away.

LIFE IN GENERAL

My overall experience of living at the ranch wasn't as bad as Janet had made it sound that it would be. The description that she programmed into my mind in forewarning me, was that it was like a jail where I would live with other "bad" and "incorrigible" boys, with the intent that maybe "they" could do something with me.

SIX FEET DEEP

Instead, I was introduced to other boys who, like myself, for one reason or another no longer lived with their parents or family. Whether we were abused, rejected, neglected, abandoned by our families, or for whatever reason that caused us to be placed at the ranch, we all had something in common...we were alone.

I quickly became accustomed to the routines at the ranch as well as to the two schools that I would attend. After all, at my age of eleven, I had already lived with several families, a children's home, a boys' home, and changed schools six times. So what was another new place to live and a couple of more new schools to attend?

BENEFITS

At a young age I had learned to become an independent person and mastered the techniques of doing laundry and skills I learned from all the chores that were assigned to me.

The biggest accomplishment I achieved came from the result from something that I wasn't expecting or even aware of, and I'm not sure of how it all originated. At some point, either through testing from the teacher at the elementary school I started attending or somewhere in my previous school records, but it was discovered that I had a reading and comprehensive deficiency.

I was enrolled into a reading skills program located on the campus of Central State College, which is now known as University of Central Oklahoma in Edmond. The results from my testing revealed that as a current sixth grader, I had the reading level as that of a child in the third grade.

For the first few months, each day after school I would walk a few blocks from the elementary school to the college and attend this program. The class sessions began with my reading a single line that was

More Prunning

projected on the wall from a machine much like an overhead projector. Each line would only consist of just a few words. This machine had a timer on it that would change the pace of the projected lines to read. Then after the completion of the short story that I read, I was given a test to show what comprehension was from what I had read.

When I began this program, the pace of the machine projected one sentence about every fifteen-seconds. As time passed and the sessions continued, the timer on this machine reduced the intervals between sentences to ten-seconds, then five-seconds, then one-second. Eventually I had progressed to only having to attend three days a week and reading a full page at a time within an allotted time.

The instructors that worked with me were like angels. Their patience, kindness, and encouragement provided within me something I had never experienced. There wasn't any yelling at me because I wasn't reading fast or comprehending fast enough as like Janet would have done to me. Instead, I began to feel extremely confident. Their long hours in tutoring and cheering me on made me feel like a giant who had just won a battle. At the end of that school year and in attending those sessions, I walked out with such a sense of accomplishment, a true achievement, and the reading and comprehension level of a ninth grader.

JANET'S THIRD VISIT

It was a Sunday afternoon in the very early spring of 1964 when Janet arrived at the ranch to visit me. She had brought along an older and balding headed man with her this time named Roger. We left campus and went into town to eat and visit. It was in no way an enjoyable time at all. Instead of enjoying each others company and making it a time of fun and laughter, the whole time we were together she harped on me about my school grades. She apparently had been keeping tabs on the grades I was making, and found this to be the unique time to spoil my day. Then to top things off, here is this older man at her side, a new and complete stranger, giving me a lecture on the importance of my need and maintaining a good education. The three hours allotted for visitation finally expired, and I thoroughly enjoyed returning to the ranch.

FINAL DAYS

School was almost over for the year when I received a letter from Janet informing me of two upcoming events. The first was to let me know that I would soon be coming back home to live with her, and the second was her announcement that she and Roger were going to be married soon.

My thoughts and emotions were mixed. My returning to live with her created questions within myself like: "How long will this last, before she sends me somewhere else?" "Will we get along or not?" "Will or relationship be like that of family or enemies?" Concerning to her marrying Roger, on one hand I wondered exactly what kind of role figure he would be for me. After all, the one and only time I met and was with him didn't leave a lasting impression with me. On the other hand, I was willing to possibly give him a chance because ever since the death of my grandpa Carl and when I was taken away from my father, there was really never a man in my life to do things together with me teaching me like how to ride a bicycle, bait a hook for fishing, build a camp fire, how to handle a pocket knife, etc. These opportunities never occurred during the time when I lived with Greg and Aubrey either, because Greg was always too busy with his remodeling project, involved with activities with his fraternal membership group, or watching television, so I learned all of these things on my own in living at boys homes. Either way, within just a few weeks I would be finding out the answers to these questions after I would return to Tulsa.

SIGNING AWAY

Next to the last day of school at the junior high school where I was

More Prunning

completing the seventh grade, I made the announcement to all of my schoolmates of my soon and planned departure in returning to Tulsa. I'm not sure why, but that particular day I wore my white dress shirt that I normally wore on Sundays to church. Before the day was over, I must have had twenty autographs and parting comments written in ink on that shirt. The next day I wore it again so for those who didn't sign it that first day, would have the chance to do so that second day. It was like having a walking yearbook autograph page on my back.

NOTES:

NOTES:

Chapter 7
A Fresh Start

My final day of living at the ranch had finally arrived. I woke up earlier than usual because I didn't sleep well, as I was fighting with mixed emotions about leaving. On one hand I was excited to be going back home to Tulsa, and yet on the other hand I was going to miss being with the other boys that I had been living and developed friendships with. I also continued to wonder what it was going to be like living with Janet again and the soon new addition of Roger.

As soon as I got up I quickly cleaned up, gathered up my personal belongings, gave away items that I didn't want, completed my chores, and began making my rounds to tell the other boys "good-bye". I'm estimating around 10:00 a.m. Janet arrived to pick me up, check me out at the administration office, and brought me back to Tulsa. After a couple of hours on the turnpike we arrived into Tulsa and onto home a few minutes later. Upon arriving at home I was immediately greeted by Aubrey and the twins - Byran and Brett.

Over the period of the next several days I experienced a familiar adjustment process. I wasn't required to perform any assigned duties, eat at designated times, and didn't have a "lights out" time at night or have to arise from bed in the mornings at a set hour. The atmosphere, attitude, and suggested comments from Janet and Aubrey were to put my life experiences and time at the ranch in the past, and try to act like it never happened.

SIX FEET DEEP

Within those first days of returning home I was also welcomed by the boys next door - John was 12 and the same age as I, Sam 11, and Pete 8. In between the times of riding our bicycles up and down the street or to a couple of convenient store that were located within a couple of blocks away in different directions, playing football, and shooting each other with homemade rubberband guns, we talked about my life and experiences at the ranch.

NEW ADDITIONS

After things settled down from the welcoming of my returning home, the focus and activities of Janet were shifted and became directed toward her upcoming marriage to Roger, which occur in just a few days. In part of the preparations for this event the twins and I were taken to some local departments stores and were bought new dress clothes for the occasion.

The big day that everyone was awaiting for had arrived. It was Saturday June 13, 1964 and the wedding was held that evening in a small church near the downtown area of Tulsa. What the future was to hold ahead of us would soon begin to unfold.

Three days later was a big deal to me as I became a teenager, and only a small celebration occurred because the newlywed couple were still on their honeymoon.

A couple of remodeling projects soon began to take place and the summer months were spent creating the combination of a new dining area and kitchen, along with a new bedroom and storage area above the single car garage. The new bedroom would eventually become mine upon completion.

A Fresh Start

SETTING A TRAP

Prior to ever meeting Janet, Roger had developed a long time friendship with the owners of the Hanging Rock Camp, which was nestled in a small wooded area and rock cliffs along side of the Illinois River in Tahlequah, Oklahoma. During that time he built pens on that property made of concrete cylinder and flat concrete blocks to raise Nutria. Nutria are a member of the rodent family, and properly said - they look like an overgrown rat.

His years of raising and breeding these Nutria had ended about a year before Roger met Janet. Now that they were married and he had gained an instant family, our trips with him to this camp were a combination of both pleasure and later into work. Pleasure came with the rental of canoes to float down the river in and/or fishing. The work involved the breaking down of the Nutria pens, trying to save the concrete blocks, and loading them in a trailer to haul back home for later use.

THE DIRTY RAT

After making a few trips to the river camp as a family outing, my trips alone with Roger began. This is where deception began. Roger had hidden a dark secret sin that he had up to this point. He began to only take me on trips to the river camp. He used this opportunity to coerce me into slowly performing sexual gratification acts. As these trips became more frequent, his expectations of these sexual pleasures became more forceful.

I didn't say anything to Janet about these incidences because 1) I felt that it would be of no use to do so; 2) I kept having the flashbacks from when Greg had me to do similar acts several years earlier, where he got mad at me for ratting on him, and how Janet never intervened; and 3) Roger's constant reminders that I was to "<u>NEVER</u> say anything to anyone about this."

FEELING USELESS

With the increasing acts of sexual violations along with the threats associated with them, I was forced to hide my emotions and live with denial. However, as time passed signs began to reveal themselves that something was wrong.

I began thinking of the friends I had developed with the boys at the ranch and how I was beginning to wish that I was still there. I missed our Sunday afternoon football games that were played on the open field of the entrance drive, going into town on Saturdays to watch movies at the theatre, and the two girlfriends that I had developed a crush on. If I would have never returned home to Tulsa and remained living at the ranch, I wouldn't be going through these experiences.

The new school year had started and once again I was attending another new school for my beginning of the eighth grade. I totally lost all interest in school, the studies of the subjects, looked forward to those last few minutes of each school day, and never completed, turned in, or studied the homework assignments. When it came time for the tests, I was usually one of the first of the students to turn them in because I never completed them and would scribble at the top of each test, "Easy F". Maybe I felt that I was helping the teacher out by his or her not having to grade them for me.

I often reflected back to the times that I took the reading courses at Central State College, the accomplishments that it achieved, and then the reality that my current life had become dirty, violated, and worthless.

VENGEANCE CAME

The sexual advancements that Roger made towards me continued

A Fresh Start

and became more frequent until something within me began to cause me to rebel as I became distant from him.

Not knowing how Janet was going to respond, the right time came along for us to talk and I nervously explained to her all that had occurred with Roger's attacks. Very much to my surprise, Janet's defense in my behalf was overwhelming to me. She carefully set the trap with the facts and Roger took the bait as when he came home from work, Janet literally planted a frying pan to the side of Roger's head and kicked him out of the house. Within a few days she filed for a divorce and on (date) 1965 their divorce was finalized.

NOTES:

NOTES:

Chapter 8
Starting Over

Almost immediately after school let out for the summer and just before my telling Janet about the sexual advancements that Roger made toward me, I took on a summer job. It was at a local family owned barbecue restaurant and located one block away from home so I could either walk or ride my bicycle. For my wages of 35 cents per hour, I started out cooking their own recipe of barbecue sauce, then later worked as a dishwasher and occasionally as a busboy.

Not only did this job create some spending money, it mainly allowed me to work some evenings and weekend hours which kept me away from Roger. It also provided me the time to plan in my mind the thoughts of how and when I'd tell Janet about Roger's advancements. After she kicked him out, I was able to quit the evening hours and work Tuesdays through Saturdays during the day.

PRIVATE TIME

When the new school year began in the fall, Janet sent the twins and me to a private school. Unknowing to her, this was a big help for me because she had me to repeat the eighth grade and by my going to another school saved me the embarrassment of seeing the previous year's classmates that I had and their knowing I was being held back. I had enough issues to deal with and didn't need the added ridicule and teasing that I may have received.

Although our daily class attendance times started at the same time, Byron and Brett got out of school each day earlier than I did. On days that weather permitted, I would load my bicycle into the back of Janet's car so I could ride it home later after school. This would prevent her from having to return to the school a second time, and it provided me some time alone to myself.

There were times while on that four and a half mile bike ride home that I just wanted to keep on riding without going home. I often thought about going back to the ranch but I figured the staff would just return me over to Janet, and that would cause things on the home front to become worse than what they already were. I also imagined myself running away to the state of California with the hope to find my father. Then reality would kick in and I knew this would be an impossibility for me to do.

BON APPETIT

Janet never had the desire or took the time to learn how to cook from her mother Aubrey. This was obvious because she didn't have the ability to cook and prepare a full course meal as examples from the meals that she dished out to us boys. Here are some examples of her meals and recipes:

Breakfast menu -
- Place a piece of bread in the toaster until it becomes dark brown in color, lightly butter and place in a bowl, pour milk over it and allow to soak. This is known as "milk toast." What can be worse than soggy toast?
- Add 1-2 teaspoons of sugar and 1 egg yolk to an 8 ounce glass, fill with milk, stir and drink. This is known as "egg nog." I like egg nog, but the real thing!
- The most frequently used and time saving meal recipe (for when short on time and on the run) was for her to have us line up, and

Starting Over

open our mouths like baby birds. Janet would then empty a cold raw egg yolk from the shell into our mouths and have us to chase this down with a small glass of milk. This was probably known as a "quickie egg nog." At least it went down quick and easy.

• For a little change in routine and create a little variety, adding 2-3 teaspoons of chocolate powder to the concoction of an egg and glass of milk for "chocolate egg nog" was occasionally provided.

Lunch menu -

• I'm still a fan for peanut butter and jelly sandwiches. But peanut butter and margarine or peanut butter and mayonnaise? No thanks.

Supper menu - aka One Course Entree' or Appetizer?

• Salad - peel off a few leaves of lettuce, rinse off under water and lightly shake off some of the access water, place on a plate and lightly sprinkle sugar over dampened lettuce, and serve.

• I still enjoy macaroni and cheese, and along with other food items. However, as a single item meal only? For growing boys? Well, bread and butter if available.

• Take a perfectly good piece of ham or steak, quickly and lightly brown on each side in a skillet, and serve alone. Either the pig will squeal or the cow will moo, and no other food items to cover the taste of raw meat.

HOUSE GUEST

I arrived home one day after school and discovered a strange car parked on the lawn in front of the house. Once inside the house Janet introduced me to Frank Webster, who was from Pomona, California. Frank was a short, older man, with dyed auburn hair that he combed straight back, a loud boisterous laugh - especially when telling his own jokes, and yet a very negative disposition that was accompanied by a permanent frown as a facial expression as though he was mad at the world all the time.

Frank was also a big blowhard in that he was always trying to impress people with a life that he really didn't have. His fortune came from inheritances that he received and certainly not from working, and whenever he introduced himself to it was, "Hi, I'm Frank G. Webster, and I'm from California." He had a need to be admired but was real obnoxious. During his two week or so stay with us, his introduction like this was given to multiple businesses as he shopped and eventually bought Janet a Baby Grand piano for a combination for her birthday and early Christmas present.

So who was this Frank Webster? It was Janet's estranged biological father whom she had not seen or had contact with for most of her life. I'm not sure who, when, or how the efforts of contact were made. However, Frank's spur of the moment of arriving in Tulsa, was the same as his departure going back to California.

FRUSTRATIONS

My adjustments at the private school was different from those I made in previous times, schools, and other places. It was very difficult for me to find anything I had in common with the other classmates. They had some beliefs within their religion that I disagreed with, and I had no problem of verbally expressing my opinions. I knew that I didn't fit in because of this, so I simply didn't try.

I became frustrated and bored as well. Because I had moved so much and never stayed in one school for any length of time, I was beginning to believe that school was just a place for babysitting, a waste of time, and I was ready to drop out. The flip side of this was I didn't want to be at home with Janet either, so I had to pick the lesser of the two evils and choosing being in school was the best escape place for me.

Starting Over
NEW STRATEGY

I didn't want to be in the position where I would have to be held back and repeat the eighth grade for a third time, so I decided that I'd do whatever it takes to prevent this from happening. I had to begin to focus on paying better attention in class, completing and turning in my homework assignments, and actually study for exams. These efforts paid off as by the end of the school year my grades were improved enough to be promoted to the ninth grade. The one thing that didn't change, was my rebellious attitude or opinion toward their religious beliefs. I think because of that, feelings were mutual in agreeing that I would not return to that school the following year or ever.

Looking back upon this time of my life, I realize I had never had help overcoming deep issues that were buried within me. There were layers of unresolved conflict and pain. I had simply shoved them down inside of me but my attitude and my behaviour was revealing my troubled life that needed healing and counsel.

Looking back at this time, people didn't open up and share with others like they do today. Also, people didn't notice signs of abuse like they do today. If someone did notice, they didn't want to get involved. Today, abuse is more recognized and talked about.

NOTES:

NOTES:

Chapter 9
Incompatabilities

I believe there are some explanations why Janet and I didn't get along. To begin with I became very independent at an early age after my having to live at the children's home and two boys homes from which I became set in my own ways. Her demanding to have things done her way, "Do as I say not as I do" attitude, and double standards at times made things even more difficult. Then of course as the main reason being the fact that I wasn't her biological son had a major affect in our relationship.

SEPARATION

During my freshman year of high school, a sense of wisdom struck me with the thought of how Janet and I could get along..."Stay away from her." She had enrolled into a Bible college that was located nearby, and her classes were during the daytime just as it was for me in school. I had taken on two newspaper routes which kept me occupied for a few hours after school and into the early evenings, then I used the latter part of the evenings to do my homework or do the subscription collections for my paper routes, while she did her studies and homework.

Along with my paper routes and school, I also started attending a church that was located a mile away from home. What a Godsend that was! I had NEVER in my life felt so loved and welcomed by a group of total strangers as the members of this church provided. I felt as though I was a long lost family member returning home for a family reunion. As an extra benefit, the girls were hot as well! Becoming actively involved with the youth department at their outings and functions was a life saver as these kept me away from the home environment.

CHRISTMAS SEASON GUEST

It wasn't Santa that showed up for the Christmas holiday this particular year, but rather Frank Webster that suddenly appeared. Again he was here to try to make his fake impressive gestures to the retailers as he had in the past. This particular year's big expense to buy his love for Janet was an organ to set near her Baby Grand piano in the living room.

Janet had a love for cats that out weighed her love for humans at times. One of her other standing house rules was "Don't mess with her cats!" Frank wasn't aware of this particular silent and golden rule of the house until the oldest of the three cats crossed his path and almost causing him to trip. As he reared back with his right leg, "Damned cat anyway!" were the words from his mouth as his leg came forward and causing the cat to go airborne. Janet just so happened to see and hear this commotion, which caused world war three to begin.

About as fast as it takes Santa to appear and disappear, Frank too had a way of making a quick vanishing act, as well as closing out this Christmas season with his comments....and they didn't sound like "Merry Christmas to all...and to all a good night!"

LOVE IS IN THE AIR

A few months into the new year had passed when word had arrived that long time family friends Duane and Doris were getting divorced, and within a short time after this, a set of new romances began - Doris met Lewis and Duane started to date Janet.

Although I'm not sure of the exact date that Doris and Lewis became

Incompatabilities

married, a year had almost passed from when Janet and Duane began dating, and they eloped during my sophomore year in high school and married on February 17, 1968.

Through the development of these relationships I became reunited with Bonita and Dan as it had been during our early elementary grade school years that we had last seen each other.

SWEET HOME CALIFORNIA!

Midway through my junior year in high school, Duane was notified by his employer that he was going to be temporarily transferred to California. This transfer would last for several months, and as a result of this his family could come along.

Girls, Beach Boys music, cars, surfing and more girls was the highlight of my teenage life while in California. When enrolling into the local high school, I was given a choice of schedules - start at 7:15 and get out at 2:45 or start at 8:45 and get out at 3:30. I didn't know why at the time but I chose the earlier schedule which proved to pay off. Getting to know the student office assistants who picked up the tardy and absentee slips at the beginning of each class had its advantages too. Usually each morning from 10:30-11:00 until 12:30 p.m. were the best times the tide came in for good surfing. My lunch period ran from 11:15-12:00, and then from 12:15-1:30 I had physical education class, which meant if I went to my last class at 1:45 with wet hair the teach never asked any questions or thought anything about it. You as the reader probably know where I'm going with this, and you've hit it dead on...a couple of other buddies of mine and I would cut our 10:15 class, the office assistants would throw away our absentee slips as us guys headed to the beach which was only fifteen minutes away, and we'd go surfing almost everyday for almost three hours.

Interestingly enough at this time I found the California school system ran about a year behind Oklahoma in their teaching curriculum. The classes I took during the second semester of my junior year in California, were the same subjects that I had taken during my sophomore year in Oklahoma. This was a great advantage for me because all of my classes served more as refreshers, and for the first time ever I made the honor roll.

WHO'S WATCHING?

I found it peculiar at times when Janet would suddenly take an unexpected exit from an interstate or turn from the major street that we would be traveling on. Then one day when this occurred, I had flashbacks from when my early years in Oklahoma because this happened quite often. I recall her telling me in those early years that someone was following her. Her present actions reminded of those from the past: suddenly speed up, run through red lights, take unexpected turns, pull into large parking lots to hide, and make turn arounds in the middle of the block. Why would someone be following her? Why live in such fear? What did she have to hide? The answers to all of these questions will later become revealed in this book.

DEAD END SEARCHES

I took advantage of living in California for nine months to search for my father. Unfortunately technology then wasn't any where advanced as it is today or in the future. Personal desktop or laptop computers, wireless phones, GPS, and internet access just didn't exist. The only reference tool that I had access to in my attempt to locate him was with the use of telephone books at the local library. I spent numerous hours on multiple occasions searching through various city directories, praying to find his name without success.

The time had arrived where the temporary work assignment for Duane had ended and for us to return to Oklahoma. I flew while Duane, Janet, and the twins traveled by car because my senior year in

Incompatabilities

high school was about to begin, and I had to leave my memories newly made friends behind.

LOCKED OUT

Late one evening during the early part of fall I was in my bedroom above the garage. I heard the voices of my neighbors John and Sam calling out my name. I went downstairs and out the back door of the garage to visit with them at the side of the house. After a short while we decided to go to one of the nearby convenience stores for a bottle of pop.

We returned home shortly and I decided to call it a night as I still had a little bit of homework to complete. I hopped over the chain linked fence and discovered the back door was locked. I found this to be odd because I knew I hadn't locked it and noticed Janet looking out the kitchen window into the backyard where I was. She came out into the garage, unlocked the door, and was yelling at me the entire time. To this day I still don't know the reason or understand what her problem was. Whatever the cause, I overheard her talking to Duane of her plans to have me made a ward of the court again.

CHRISTMAS PACKING

After the incident involving my going to the convenience store that one evening, I had decided to initiate plans to move out. I knew to do this I needed to complete my senior year, graduate, and save up enough money for an apartment.

I took advantage of the Christmas break from school by packing up some of my belongings and keeping them in my closet and the attic. Then over the course of the next few months, I'd slip in empty boxes and continue to slowly pack items that I didn't have immediate need of.

SIX FEET DEEP
NO PEAS PLEASE

My high school graduation commencement ceremony was just a few days away. I was standing in the front yard next door talking with John, Sam, and Pete when one of us suggested going to the convenience store. We all walked to the store, bought the items we went after, and returned to the front yard of their home. Several minutes went by before Janet stepped out onto our front porch and hollered out my name to let me know supper was ready. I could tell by the tone of her voice that something was about to go down. "Ah...the convenience store thing again" I thought to myself.

Sure enough, when I walked in the door, "Just where the hell have you been?" she yelled out, "I've called out to you three times to get in here for dinner."

Me: "I went to the store and got a pop with John, Sam, and Pete."

Janet: "Well you could have had the decency to come in and told me."

Me: "All I did was just go to the store to get a bottle of pop!" "I was only gone a few minutes."

Janet: "Well from now on you are to come and check in with me."

Me: "No I will not! I'm 18 years old, I'll be graduating from high school in just a few days, and I'll be 19 in a few weeks. I have a job and will come and go as I please, and I'm not going to ask for mommy's permission to go to the store, and be treated like a small child."

Janet: " Well your dad (referring to Duane) comes and tells me when he leaves to go somewhere."

Me: "Yeah and that's a different relationship too, you're not my wife."

Incompatabilities

Janet: " Well let me just tell you this, IF you ever get married and you ever treat your wife like you do me, don't you be surprised if you find yourself standing in front of a judge getting a divorce."

Me: "Well I can top that."

Janet: "All your life I've told you of things that would happen to you, and I've always been right." "Now what is it that's so important that you've got to say?"

Me: "If my wife ever acts like you, I'll find my self standing in front of the judge every day!"

As she was making her last say, I was serving myself some peas onto my plate. After I made my last remark, she immediately walked over to where I was sitting, picked up the plate, she cursed me as she broke the plate over my head and the peas flew everywhere. I stood up with my fist clinched and wanted to just knock her out so bad, but didn't. Instead I scooped up a handful of peas off the floor, and as I threw them across the table, I looked at her with the hatred that I held within and said, "I will never eat supper in this house again!"

Not wanting to EVEN be in the same house with her, I went upstairs to my room, changed clothes, and left to go to my girlfriend's house. I'm really surprised that I didn't break the glass or the storm door itself when I slammed it going out. Unresolved hurts and anger were mounting within my heart.

In route to my girlfriend's house, what echoed in my thoughts over and over was Janet's last commanding comment, "Now then you little smart aleck bastard, clean up your mess...clean up your mess...clean up your mess." Okay, so she picks up a plate of food, hits ME over the head, and now it's MY mess?! Wow!

SIX FEET DEEP

I initially had a date that evening but because of my horrible headache along with a knot about the size of a golf ball on top of my head, we agreed to just stay at her home and watch television.

DAY OF FREEDOM

There's an old cliche and a song entitled "Silence is Golden" which was like music to my ears because that's the way it was around the home front over the next few days. Janet finally broke the silence informing me that if I wanted to have my clothes washed I'd have to pay her for the water, or if I wanted to eat I'd have to pay her for the food. I never responded back but I sure put my thoughts into motion. So for the next few days I didn't put my clothes in the clothes hamper to be washed and I ate out.

I came home after work a couple of days later and greeted the women in Janet's Bible study that she often had. This was ironic since I never knew that Janet ever truly accepted Jesus as Lord and Savior. "Oh hi honey" I heard Janet say, but I didn't acknowledge her and went about my business. Within just a few minutes I walked out with my first full box of belongings. After about the fourth or fifth trip of coming in empty handed and carrying boxes out, she excused herself as I came in. With a fake grin, showing her teeth, and her jaws clinched she asked me, "Just what in the H-E-double L do you think you are doing?" In my regular tone of voice I replied back, "Oh, I forgot to tell you. I'm moving out." I gave her and the other women a big smile, and went for my next box. Although it wasn't planned, I couldn't have picked a better day or a more perfect time to carry out my plan for moving.

Chapter 10
Times of Hardship

Two years had passed since I graduated from high school and moved out on my own. My girlfriend and I began having problems with our relationship as for several months we would break up, get back together, break up, etc. We were serious enough that we wanted to get married as I had bought the rings, she had her maid-of-honor and bridesmaids selected, the colors picked, and we even had a date chosen. However, because she was a senior at the time her parents wanting her to go to college after high school, and our several months of bickering, her parents put their foot down on not allowing her become engaged to me.

We had been broken up throughout the summer and when fall arrived she moved to Mississippi to attend college and I started attending a local junior college to major in Police Science, as my life ambition was to have a career as a police officer.

Toward the end of October I received a letter from my ex-girlfriend informing that she was coming home for the Thanksgiving holiday and wanted to see me. I became so thrilled that I couldn't keep her off my mind. It was almost like when we first met and started going steady. I guess one could repeat the old saying that, "Distance makes the heart grow fonder."

As time became closer to Thanksgiving, I began to focus my thoughts on her coming home and how I wanted to make a lasting impression on her. My first plan was to sell my car because one of the areas that we had difficulty with in our relationship was my over car. There were times I spent more money on fixing up my car for racing than I did dating her.

Three days before she came home I traded in my "hotrod" car for one that I'd tag as a "grandma's" car. It was a pretty car if you like gold metallic paint versus silver, gold cloth with silk stitching seats versus burgundy leather, white wall tires versus raised white lettering, hubcaps versus chrome mag wheels, an automatic transmission versus a four speed stick shift, and a quiet stock muffler versus headers and glass packs.

My first day of ownership of this new set of wheels was miserable. What had I done? I purposely stayed hidden from all of my friends because I didn't want to be seen inside this car or behind the wheel, and get ridiculed by them. On my second day I tried to think with the mindset of a matured young man, acknowledging that we at times have to make sacrifices for those we love, and there was purpose for what I was doing. The third day came and all I could think of was her and I meeting for lunch, proving myself to her with my maturity…and… buying a different car, and then of course our getting back together.

I had great difficulty staying focused on my job and instead kept track of the time and looking out the window for her arrival in the parking lot. When she became one minute late my heart began to beat a little faster. At fifteen minutes late I became fearful. At thirty minutes late I began to panic. Finally after an hour later my heart began to sink. I called her home telephone number numerous times, leaving messages both with her mother and sister. After making numerous calls the next day on Thanksgiving, leaving the same messages, and not receiving a returned call, I knew I was had…stuck with a gold car and thought to myself, "I'm not so mature after all."

The following Monday I went to the car lot to tell them I had changed my mind and wanted my old car back. However, upon my arrival I didn't

Times of Hardship

see "hotrod" anywhere in the parking lot and was later informed that it had been sold.

A few days later I received a letter from my ex-girlfriend, apologizing that she wasn't able to meet me for lunch...because...she went out with a guy who she met the summer before, he proposed to her, and she accepted. I was literally crushed.

HAPPY HOLIDAYS?

My streak of bad luck at the beginning of the holiday season had only just begun. When Christmas cards at work were passed out, I became secretly excited with the anticipation of receiving a bonus. Instead it was a pink slip...I was being laid-off.

Over the period of the next couple of weeks, I started my new year off with being laid-off from work, evicted from my apartment because I didn't have enough money to pay rent, and someone wanted the gold car more than me. It was found a few days later in an abandoned field stripped and burned.

The finance company informed me they had found a clause in my auto insurance policy that made a provision for a rental car. I was sent to a particular dealership and within an hour or so I was driving off in a new car.

I had made friendships with several police officers over the past several months. One in particular had heard of the problems that I was experiencing and offered to let me temporarily stay in his garage apartment for free until he could make it rentable and allow me to get back on my feet financially. He also later helped me get hired at a security company where the owner was a close friend of his.

SIX FEET DEEP

WEDDING SORROWS

After I moved into the garage apartment, tragedy almost happened. It was a Saturday evening at 7:30, a wedding was about to take place in a church that I was well familiar with. I knew the maid-of-honor, the names of all the bridesmaids, and even the colors chosen. Who I didn't know was the groom to be, his best man, or the groomsmen. It was the wedding of my former girlfriend and her fiance.

I started drinking alcohol earlier that afternoon to try to drown my sorrows of this known event. After having several drinks and beginning to feel tipsy, I drove over to the church, stood at the front entrance, stared through the pane glass windows, and began to weep as I watched glimpses of the ceremony.

The effects of the amount of alcohol I had consumed were beginning to hit me harder, so I left and drove my way back to the garage apartment. Inside I continued to drink, weep, and tried to reason out why it wasn't me instead this other guy that was getting married. After all, he had only known her for a few months, whereas I knew and went steady with her for three years.

I woke up the next morning sprawled out on the single bed, with my loaded and cocked .38 caliber pistol in my hand, my right index finger through the trigger guard and almost resting against the trigger, and the barrel pointing toward the right side of my head. Apparently I had drowned myself so deep in my pool of sorrows and alcohol that I contemplated committing suicide and passed out instead. I'm truly thankful for God's love and grace which was shown through my becoming incoherent and His saving of my life.

LEGAL PROBLEM

A few days later I was asked- to move in with a friend Joe along with

Times of Hardship

his mother Betty and sister Sandy because they were concerned about me after of my suicide attempt. I thought things were about to look up for me because I had been hired by the police officer's friend who owned the security company. I bought the required uniform and had to wait for the alterations to be completed. A few days later I picked up the uniform and was excited about getting to start work that evening. I arrived back at my friend's apartment to take a quick nap and then get ready to start my job.

After waking up from my nap and preparing to take a shower, I realized that I had left my new uniform in the car. As I walked outside and going toward the car I saw a woman walking toward another car nearby that was occupied by another women. It almost appeared that the first woman had been looking through the windows of my rental car when I startled her coming outside. No conversation was exchanged and I went about my business.

Within fifteen to twenty minutes later, the door bell rang and Sandy called out my name saying someone was at the door looking for me. I came downstairs and was greeted by a man dressed in a suit. He asked for confirmation of my name, introduced himself as a detective, and had a warrant for my arrest on a felony charge of Embezzlement by Bailee. I asked him to repeat the charge because he might as well had spoken Greek to me. A nearby uniformed officer came forward, informed me I was under arrest, placed handcuffs on my wrists, and escorted me to his patrol car. As we were walking to his car, I looked around and noticed several uniformed and plain clothed police officers that had surrounded the apartment, along with the same two women that I had just seen moments earlier checking out my rental car.

During the time I was being transported to the police station I asked the police officer what these charges meant. "Embezzlement" to my knowledge was like someone stealing from their employer. I wasn't employed and knew I hadn't stolen anything from any previous employers. "Bailee" was a term I had never heard of before. It almost sounded like posting bail. Putting those together made it sound like I had stole something from a person who had posted bail. The officer expressed his lack of knowledge or understanding as well.

I was placed in a holding cell along with several other offenders waiting to be booked and processed. Roughly an hour passed and I had a sudden need to go to the bathroom. I called out to an officer a couple of times expressing my need and was ignored. On the third time I yelled out louder and he responded back in a snapping way, "Shut up and go in the corner!" I did as he instructed. Approximately thirty minutes later a couple of other officers came in and called out my name. I responded, and they roughed me up a little with their slapsticks because I had relieved myself in the corner. They told me to clean up my mess with the towels they threw at me, and took me to be officially booked and processed. After being processed I was allowed to make my "one" telephone call. I called Janet to explain what happened, and her response was, "Well, it sounds like you're on your own." Then she hung up. I was then escorted to a cell in the city jail where I joined two other offenders.

The following morning I was transferred to the county jail and placed in a cell that held the capacity of twelve offenders but had eight other offenders at the time. One of these eight wasn't present until later that day because he was at the hospital being treated for the injuries he acquired during a fight the night before with one of the other offenders in this cell. The other offender involved had earlier been treated and released with a broken nose and a black eye.

I was able to make a couple of phone calls later in the day in my attempts to reach an attorney that I knew as well as one that was friend of Duane. In both cases, they required fees that I didn't have and both suggested that I contact a public defender.

Times of Hardship

After a week or so had passed, I received the following letter:

Apr. 24, 1973

Steve :

You probably know this by now having I supposed talked with the Public Defender, but if you were bailed out, you would not be eligible for the services of the Public Defender. And it is required to pay an attorney in advance for services rendered in a criminal matter. Consequently, if you were bailed out with $100 which is 10% of the bail, you would then find yourself with no attorney to represent you, so legally as well as morally, you are actually better off where you are. I regret not coming to see you, but in all honesty, I just don't want to see you. I am sad by what has happened, but I guess you have had time to think of some things I've said and where you would end, and that the time would come when I could not help you even if I wanted to. You have reached that place. You have the charm, the personality, and the wit to have become anything you wanted, and you've had the opportunity, but this is what you have chosen; the company you've kept, the using of people, in the end payday comes. I have done, and the rest of the family has done everything humanly possible to help you and there has been no lack of love. If you had used your talents in a lawful manner you could have been an unqualified success. Instead, you're just a cheap crook. Don't forget you chose the way. I am not sympathetic and I do not care to hear any more of your lies and conning tactics. I am sad for the man who could have been, and isn't. Such a waste. Do you remember the story I told you when your were only 7 years old? About the little boy who tended the sheep and thought it would be funny to cry "wolf" and the people from the town all ran out to save the flock from the wolf and the boy laughed and laughed when they came and there was no wolf. And he even tried it a second time and the people came to help him and there was no wolf. But one day the wolf really came and the boy cried "wolf" and cried and cried, but the people thought he was tricking them again and no one came and the wolf attacked the flock and the boy. You have cried wolf many times and we've all come running to help, and you've laughed behind our backs at how you worked us for what you wanted. But this time, ...

have you noticed no one is coming. And this time you are really in trouble. Where are your wonderful friends? Are they flocking round to pay the bail and get and attorney for you.
The waste of you is what makes me so sad."

My first thoughts after receiving this letter were to keep it in a safe place, and when the time comes that Janet dies, I will toss this letter in her grave, and relieve myself over her casket as it's being lowered into the ground. My bottled up feelings of bitterness and hatred for Janet had just begun to pour out.

For the next day or so I really never thought of the legal case and issue that I was in, instead I had flashbacks from all the earlier years in my life and then questioned some of her comments in the letter. I re-visioned the times I was made to sit in a bathroom with my feet and hands tied up with rope, sexually abused by Greg, cussed at, beat on, spit on, slapped, sent off to boys homes, sexually abused by Roger on multiple occasions, and hit over my head with a plate. Where does *"...the rest of the family has done everything humanly possible to help you and there has been no lack of love"* fit in?

What I later learned was, the rental agreement that I signed at the dealership stated I was to be provided a free rental car for thirty days. Any time beyond that period, I would be held liable for any accrued daily rental fees. I had the car for ninety days. With my age of twenty-two years old at the time and possibly my lack of knowledge of legal documents, I didn't pay attention to any of these time issue requirements, and this is what caused me to get into this legal mess. Apparently this qualified me to be in Janet's eyes, *"...just a cheap crook."*

BLOCKED ATTEMPTS

I was informed about a bonding program that I was eligible for. This program would allow me to be released without paying the required

Times of Hardship

10%, as like other bail bonds , instead I'd have a set of rules to abide by including a 10:00 PM curfew, no use of illegal drugs or alcoholic drinks, and reporting to a probation officer on a weekly basis. I made application, met with representatives from this program, approved, and was well set to be released within a matter of a few days. Without any advanced notice, my application was abruptly denied and withdrawn.

I learned that Janet had contacted the attorney she used for adopting me, requested that he keep tabs on my case, and keep her informed of the proceedings regarding my case. When she heard that I was about to be released under this bonding program, she contacted the program firm and told them if they released me that I had plans to run off to California. Where she came up with this idea is beyond me.

BLACK SHEEP

My opinion of public defenders was that they are in an internship position of practicing law, and were there to just collect a check win, lose, or draw. However, the one assigned to me by the courts was a godsend. He truly expressed his interest in my case, applied his expertise in a very professional way, and a few years later opened up his own law firm.

The date of my trial had arrived. Under my public defender's orders I appeared in court cleanly shaved and my hair neatly combed. I even went the extra mile by dampening my county issued inmate shirt a few days earlier, and placed it under my mattress to let dry, giving it a fresh ironed look.

As I sat in the assigned section where other offenders awaited for their cases to be called, I began to shake like a leaf on a windy day. My public defender came over and whispered in my ear, "Why are you so intensely shaking? Are you cold or nervous?" I told him that it must be from being nervous. "Don't worry" he said, "I have a plan."

SIX FEET DEEP

My name was called out and I was motioned by my public defender to remain sitting. He went forward and asked the judge if they could have a private meeting in the judge's chamber. Several minutes passed and my anxiety was growing. The door from the judge's chamber opened, my public defender came and sat next to me, and whispered, " We've been offered a deal. If you plead guilty, you'll get a year's probation, and I can get you out of here."

Me: "Guilty? I'm not guilty! I didn't do anything."

PD: "Well if you don't take this deal, you're looking at spending five to ten years in prison." "So I'm telling you, you better take it, and you'll be released from here."

Me: "When you say that you'll get me out and I'll be released, how long of time are you talking about?"

PD: "You'll be out of here within twenty-four hours."

Me: "Okay, I'll do it."

He got up and went back into the judge's chamber. A few minutes later he and the judge entered the court room and I was motioned to come forward.

Judge G reminded me of the character that played the lion in the classic movie Wizard of Oz. He could occasionally offer a small smile but could quickly offer an expression of anger with the snap of a finger if needed. His opening remarks to me with, "Young man, it's been presented to me that this is the first time you've been in trouble with the law. Is this correct?"

Me: "Yes Sir."

Times of Hardship

Judge G: "I also understand there appears to be a strain in the relationship between you and your family. Would you agree to say this is a fair conclusion?"

Me: "Yes Sir."

Judge G: "It's almost as though you're being treated as the black sheep of the family. Wouldn't you agree?"

Me: "Yes Sir."

Judge G: "I see. Do you understand the case that is being presented before you?"

Me: "Yes your Honor"

Judge G: "And do you understand the consequences that you are facing?"

Me: "Yes Sir."

Judge G: "And what is your plea?"

Me: "Guilty your Honor."

Judge G: "With your understanding and plea before this court, I hereby sentence you to one year of probation. At the end of that one year, you are to appear here here in court, and if I see a satisfactory report to the courts of your actions, I will expunge your records. However, if I see or hear of you violating any as even one of the terms of this probation granted to you, I will revoke your probation and you serve the remaining amount of time in prison as the law allows. Do you understand this?"

SIX FEET DEEP

Me: "Yes Sir, your Honor."

Judge G: "I don't want to see you in my court again, for any reason, until next year. Have a good day young man."

Me: "Yes Sir. Thank you."

The gavel came down making it's loud crashing sound. I was excused and met with my public defender outside of the court room. I thanked him as he patted me on the shoulder, and told me he'd start processing my release immediately.

The next morning I woke up early with excitement and anticipation of being released. My only last wish for there was they'd serve cinnamon rolls for breakfast as that was about the only desired food item that was ever served during my thirteen weeks of being incarcerated. Behold my unrequested wish was granted, as when the "bean hole" door was opened, black coffee and cinnamon rolls was served. I received this as an early reminder that this particular day was going to be great.

As I came closer to the double doors to exit from the county jail building, I slowly began to exhale all the breath that was in me. The moment I stepped outside, I quickly lunged forward and took in a deep breath of fresh air. I noticed the scent of honey suckle in the air and for a moment thought I had died and gone to heaven. I recall looking straight up at the beautiful blue sky and saying, "God, you will never see me in a place like this again." Never in my wildest or deepest imaginations did I ever think this would ever occur again. However, look at me today, frequently going into jails and prisons around the world ministering to incarcerated men and women and presenting them the Word of God.

I've learned to never say never to God, because He has a better plan in mind.

Chapter 11
Starting Over Again

I was so excited about being released from jail that I didn't mind walking the nine and a half miles to get to the apartment where I was staying earlier. Breathing fresh air, seeing green grass and blooming flowers during my walk was a treat for me. Before arriving to the apartment, I stopped by the post office where I had my mail delivered to. It was packed with mostly sales ads but I saw an envelope that made my face light up. It was a brown envelope containing my income tax refund check. Hallelujah! Each moment upon my release was getting better.

As the next several months passed by I arranged and made monthly payments to the dealership for the rental car fees I owed, had gotten a job, bought a used car, met my daily curfew, fulfilled my probation requirements, and reported to my probation officer each month.

I recall the first time I went into the dealership to make the arrangements and how strained the relationship was. To my surprise the tension broke rather quickly. The woman who I dealt with from the very beginning was apologetic that this matter went as far as it did, because it wasn't her or the dealership's intention to have me arrested with a felony charge and go to jail. She told me of a previous conversation where Janet told her I was moving to California. Since this woman didn't have any other way of contacting me at the time, she and the dealership had no other alternative but to use legal means of retrieving their rental car, regardless of what it took or the outcome.

SIX FEET DEEP

My year of probation had expired and I appeared in court on the date assigned to me by Judge G with my public defender at my side. Judge G wasn't in a good mood, most likely due to the previous case he had just ruled over. He viewed over my file, looked at me with a quick glance, and back at my file. We had a short conversation where he asked for my receipts for paying the restitution amount due to the dealership. I provided him with those receipts along with a letter from the woman who I dealt with at the dealership.

"I've reviewed the report from your probation officer and commend you for your efforts in fulfilling the orders of this court by successfully completing the terms of your probation requirements and the paying in full the amount of restitution" he said. "As stated in your case trial, if you met these requirements without any further incident, I would expunge your records regarding this matter. You have met and fulfilled these requirements as ordered and I order your records to be expunged by this court." "Do you have any questions?" I answered, "No your Honor I don't." He responded back, "Don't let me see you back in my court." With a big smile he looked at me and winked.

COMMUNICATION CYCLE RETURNS

As described in an earlier chapter, the cycles of communications and silence with Janet returned. Her initial efforts of breaking the silence were identical as the ones in the past with declarations of her concern of my well being and as if nothing had ever caused problems and separations between us. I don't know why I always gave in but I obviously was weak in this area. However, our relationship and communications never became close or as frequent again, as I remained distant and with my guard up.

LIFE'S A PARTY

Over the next few years I experienced a short term and failed

Starting Over Again

marriage along with a live-in relationship of another woman, and employment with a beer distributor as a route sales representative. At first I took advantage of all the entertainment, parties, and so called friendships that had developed. However after a few years of this life style, it was beginning to take a toll on me. There were plenty of early mornings where I was still drunk and/or suffering from a hangover, go home to my apartment just in time to change clothes, go to work, check the inventory of beer on my truck, and be in route to my first stop at 6:00. Usually around noon I began to feel like I was back into the human race and ready to carry out the rest of the day, promising myself that when I got off work, "No partying tonight." The "no partying" rarely happened because invariably at the end of the workday there were always other employees informing all of us of a special event, occasion, party, or celebration being held at one of their accounts. There was an unwritten requirement in our job descriptions in that we were to show our "Public Relations" by attending these events. Therefore this cycle of working all day and partying all night became non-ending lifestyle for me...day in and day out.

A TIME FOR CHANGE

I had reached a point in my life that I was beginning to get tired of this partying lifestyle. I wanted out of the live-in relationship with the girlfriend I had developed, but didn't know how to go about it. I've always hated to see women cry, especially if I was the one wanting to break up.

My live-in girlfriend wanted to go out one weekend evening with some of her girl friends. There weren't any scheduled events or parties going on for me and I decided to stay home. I fumbled with the cable box by rolling the row selector and pushing the buttons to select a channel in my efforts to find something to watch on television. Punching one button after another and on the last of the three rows to select from, I was now tuned in to a religious program with a well known minister who was preaching in a baseball stadium. I became glued to some of his closing sermon comments. I then began to have flashbacks and old memories of the church involvement I had during my high school years. During the closing "altar call" moments of the television program I started to reason with myself and God. I made a verbal promise to Him that if He would cause my live-in girlfriend and I to break up, but most importantly that she do the breaking up so that I didn't have to see her cry, in return I would turn my life around and get back on track with Him.

A few weeks had past and no changes in our relationship occurred, so I figured that God didn't really care about my situation and I continued living in the same environment that I was in, and two months later we bought a house together.

We had been in our new home a month and a half when one evening she told me that she wanted to treat us to dinner as she wanted to talk to me. We went to a nearby steakhouse, enjoyed a good meal, and she expressed her emotions of being unhappy and wanted to break our relationship off. I was a little hurt but more mad over the idea of our recently buying the house together.

Two and a half months later, on a Friday afternoon, I was on the way back to the distributor warehouse in the tractor-trailer rig that I drove when I heard an audible voice say, "You have made me a promise that you have not kept." I became so startled that I immediately grabbed the air brake handle on the steering column along with stomping down on the foot brake pedal and fought to keep from jackknifing the rig as I pulled over to the shoulder of the road. Totally broken out in a sweat and panting like a dog, I sat there for several minutes to gain my normal composure back. There was no doubt whose voice I had heard and what promise He was referring to.

When I arrived to the warehouse to check in my truck and its

Starting Over Again

inventory, I was asked by a few of my coworkers if I was feeling all right. When I confirmed that I was, I asked "Why?" Their responses back were "You look shaken up over something."-OR "You look like you've seen a ghost." I knew what the true answer was but didn't reveal this information, turned down the going to a party, and went home for a quiet weekend.

TURNING OVER A NEW LEAF

That Sunday morning I returned to the church that I had attended during my high school years. I was welcomed by many of the familiar faces of members who remembered me from my earlier years as well as from some old friends. A young couple who were about my age had just recently taken over the position of senior pastors of the church as the founding pastor was close to retiring. I was introduced to this new young pastor just before the beginning of the morning service. I recall him looking at me straight in eye and his revealing to me things of my life that occurred in the past. I was overwhelmed at his knowledge and thought to myself, "Wow, there must be a billboard that's lit up and pointing down on me that he's reading from." How in the world did he know these things?

During the altar call at the end of that service, I went down to the altar and surrendered my entire life over to God. I felt so refreshed afterwards. All the heaviness from burdens that I had been carrying was lifted and taken from me. I returned that evening for another dose of blessings from heaven with the teaching (not preaching) style that this young pastor had, along with the worship and fellowship this church had.

The following morning I went to work totally refreshed. No hangover, no headache, and full of new energy. Both some of my coworkers and customers noticed a change in me put couldn't figure it out. Some tried to guess with suggestions including I must have found a new girlfriend,

SIX FEET DEEP

but none could guess the correct answer. As the day progressed, I began to feel uncomfortable inside. I couldn't fully describe it or even put a finger on it until later that evening. After work and arriving to my apartment, I realized when opening the refrigerator and cabinets, I had no food other than a few bags of chips, a container of dip or two, and a large amount beer, including an old 1950's style refrigerator that I had converted into a keg box with a full keg of beer inside. It was at that moment that I realized that the reason I felt uncomfortable inside was because I had given my life to the Lord the day before. This new life of Christ in me and working in the beer industry didn't and wouldn't mix. It was time to move on.

GIVE IT ALL UP

The next morning I went to work with the intentions of resigning from my job. However about half way there, I convinced myself that I couldn't until I found another job. I dealt with reasoning to myself over and over for the next couple of days, trying to rationalize both sides of this argument. It reminded me of the old cartoons that I watched as child where an angel stood on the left shoulder providing instructions while a red devil on the right shoulder providing arguments and excuses.

The walls in my apartment were decorated with coveted beer advertisement lights, plaques, and pictures along with a lighted pool table light hanging from the ceiling over my dining room table. I pulled all of these items off the walls and ceiling, disposing all but one into the dumpster outside in the parking lot. The one I kept had lights in it with a halo-graphic foil that when lit up produced multiple colors through the painted design on the front glass. I later scratched off the painted design, drew and painted the name of Jesus in the shape of a dove, and still own this item to this day.

After I returned to the warehouse at the end of that Friday, I checked in my truck with my remaining inventory, turned in my counted sales ticket

Starting Over Again

receipts and money, and gave my written resignation to my supervisor effective immediately. The little angel on my left shoulder won!

NOTES:

NOTES:

Chapter 12
Making Adjustments

Although I wasn't used to being unemployed and moving around in a slower pace, it was relaxing to sleep in those first few mornings without having to go to work during the early morning hours and smell the scent of beer.

I also wasn't used to staying home with my previous lifestyle so going to church for the two services on Sundays and one on Wednesday evening gave me something to look forward to. My involvement with the singles ministry and attending their weekly prayer meeting also helped occupy my time. During the day I was able to do some odd and end part-time jobs to pay my rent and buy a few groceries.

RECEIVING THE CALL

I owned a triple white 1976 Pontiac Grand Prix that was so cold natured, I often had to stay with it quite a while on cold mornings until the engine would idle on its own. I always kept a spare key to it for these times for once it would continue to idle, I could turn up the heater and/or defroster to full blast, and lock the car while I returned to my apartment to finish getting dressed. Then I'd use the spare key to get back into my now toasty warm car.

Sunday December 9,1979 was one of those cold mornings that the car needed my babysitting assistance. There was a little snow on the ground, frost on the windshield, and with every step I walked toward the car, I could hear the grass crunch because of the ice. As I sat inside dressed in a pair of slacks, a T-shirt, and house shoes while trying to keep the engine idling, I watched my breath fog up the inside of all the windows.

I then heard a voice saying, "I'm calling you into the ministry." Then it was silent again. I thought it was coming from the radio station that I normally listened to, so I reached over to turn up the volume only to discover the radio wasn't even turned on. I moved my eyes from side to side and thought, "Ohhh boy." A minute or so passed and I heard the voice again saying, "Steve, I'm calling you into the ministry." I then spoke out and said, "Oh God, if that's you, you've got the wrong person. I don't know anything about being a preacher, I don't even know enough about the Bible to even become a preacher, and besides, I can't talk in front of a group of people." Total silence. I then looked around to make sure no one was watching some guy out in a cold car and sitting there talking to himself.

The engine had warmed up to idle on its own and I returned to my apartment and finished getting dressed. I returned to my car, turned "on" the radio so I could hear and sing along with some of the music, and off to church I went. The moment I put the gear selector into "Park" and about to turn off the ignition switch, again I heard that voice say in a little louder tone, "I'm calling you into the ministry."

CONFIRMATION

I felt so flustered inside because of this experience of hearing this voice, I decided that instead of sitting where I normally did, I would to sit in the balcony since not very many people sat there and I wanted to be alone. Wrong! On this particular morning's service the sanctuary became packed out, including the balcony where I was.

I have no idea what my pastor spoke on that morning because I couldn't get this voice experience out of my thoughts along with

Making Adjustments

the warm radiant feeling in my chest. When the service was over I immediately began making my way to the parking lot. The exit door to the parking lot is where the pastor and his wife always stood to visit with the members as they left. Pastor D was already talking with a couple as I approached that area and I side stepped around them to avoid any interruption. The moment I was within a few feet from him, he excused himself from talking with that couple, and called out my name. Looking at me straight in the eye and using his right index finger to lightly tap on my chest he said, "Steve, the Lord is calling you into the ministry and you need to be obedient." Standing there, I know my lower jaw had to drop open and hit the floor. "How did you know this?" I asked, "This just happened a couple of hours ago!" His reply was, "The Lord has revealed this to me, and I'm confirming with you." I continued to give him the same excuses I gave God earlier why I couldn't. He looked at me and said, "Just be obedient."

LOOK ALIKE

I can't recall who the special-guest speaker scheduled for that evening was, but it was one who was well known and I knew if I wanted to have a good seat that I needed to arrive earlier than usual, so I did just that. I placed my Bible at the end of the pew where I wanted to sit, and wondered around the building until more people would begin to arrive. At the front of the foyer area is long straight way with floor to ceiling pane glass windows that over looks the main street. I had just got a drink from the water fountain, turned around, and started looking out those windows watching the traffic pass by when I was approached by another gentleman. "So" he says, "Are you the guest preacher tonight?" "Excuse me?" I asked. "I was wondering if you are the preacher that's coming in tonight?" "No, why do you ask?" I answered. "Well, you look like the preacher type, and the way you're dressed, I just thought you were him." "Here we go again" I thought to myself. A bit choked up, I thanked him and he turned around and walked away. I had never seen this man before, and to my knowledge, I've never seen him again.

SIX FEET DEEP

As a side note, I no longer have that particular suit anymore (you know how those dry cleaners will cause your clothes to shrink) but I still own the tie I wore.

INVITATION

After the service the following Sunday evening, Pastor D called me off to the side and asked if I recalled the discussion we had the previous Sunday morning. "Do I ever!" I stated. I shared with him that it was like my whole week was ruined (but not in a negative way) in that the entire week had been consumed with all those thoughts, incidents, and discussions about my being called into the ministry, and how I can't seem to escape it.

He then asked, "You do know we started a new Bible school this year here, correct?" I acknowledged that I had heard about it. He then said, "Well this coming week is the last week for this semester before closing for the Christmas holiday break. I want you to sit in all the classes throughout this week, and later on tell me what you think of it." I nodded my head and agreed to do so.

The following morning I started attending the classes as agreed, and did so for the four hours each day. I thoroughly enjoyed the teachings and amazed with the presence of God that was there. It was almost like being in a one-week revival.

Three weeks later Pastor D asked me if I attended the school and what I thought of it. I confirmed that I had, and shared my thoughts and opinion of the school. "Good." He said. " The new semester starts tomorrow morning and I want you to be there to start full-time." I'm sure I looked at him with a little bit of a confused facial expression and said, "Well, I don't know." He then asked, "What do you mean you don't know? Didn't you share with me that one of the reasons you told the Lord why you couldn't become a minister is because you don't know enough

Making Adjustments

about the Bible?" "Yes." I replied. "How else are you going to learn about the Bible if you don't go to school to do so?" He had me! "Well, I'm sure there's a cost to attend this school." I said. He said, "Yes." And then stood there in silence. I then said, "Well I don't think you understand. I don't have the money it's going to cost, my car is broke down, my rent is due, and I don't have a steady job." He looked at me for a moment and said, "No, I think it's you that don't understand. You've been called into the ministry. It's a level where God wants you to be. When God guides, He provides." I was overwhelmed with that last statement, "When God guides, He provides." I had never heard that before, and it just kept echoing in my head. I agreed to enroll and start attending.

GOD'S PROVISION

I was given a ride home that evening by a friend who lived fairly close to me. On the way home I shared the discussion that I just had with Pastor D regarding Bible school. Just as we arrived to my apartment complex my friend offered to give me a ride to school each morning if I could find a ride home, and I accepted.

The following morning I kept my promise in enrolling into the Bible school and thoroughly absorbed the teachings the instructors offered. After arriving home early that afternoon, I found an envelope taped to my apartment door. I thought to myself, "Oh great. An eviction notice from the apartment manager's office." As I opened up the door my telephone began ringing so I laid the envelope on the bar and went to answer the telephone.

The next day after coming home from school, I found another envelope taped to the door. I opened it up when I got inside, and sure enough if was a notice from the manager's office reminding me that my rent was past due. Then I remembered that I never opened the first envelope. I opened it and found four $100 currency bills inside without any note or explanation. This gave me enough to pay my month's rent, telephone,

SIX FEET DEEP

electric, and a few groceries. "God is my provider." I yelled out loud.

I continued to attend Bible school that entire second semester, then came back in the fall and completed the first semester, and waited for that class to complete their second semester for graduation. In the meantime I gained full time employment to pay for my rent and bills, and the Lord miraculously provided in paying my all of my tuition fees and costs of books for my education. "When God guides, He provides."

NOTES:

Chapter 13
Fulfilling the Birthday Wish

While I waited for the current Bible school class to complete the second semester and graduate, I began to have the opportunity to minister in a few churches on the weekends in surrounding towns as well as locally through the assistance of another minister friend of mine.

At one of these churches I made eye contact with a young woman that caught my attention. A few weeks later I had just come home from work and noticed a young woman was staring at her car with the hood up because it wouldn't start. I asked if I could assist her, and when she turned around, low and behold it was the same young woman who I had seen at the church earlier. Both of us were a little surprised acting at first, and neither one of us knew what to say at first. I excused myself to leave long enough to change clothes and came back. As I added water to the battery gave it a jump start, I learned that she lived in the building across from my apartment at the opposite end. She thanked me, introduced herself as Freda, and explained that she had to leave to go join her mother and grandmother for dinner.

A few hours later she returned while I was outside my apartment door cooking my supper on the grill. We started to visit and a little later took an evening stroll through the campus of a nearby university. In our discussions, she told me that her life had some similar situations as mine. She also grew up with a broken home as her father, although a good man, was an alcoholic, beat her mother when he came home drunk, and they later divorced. Her mother moved to California for a

SIX FEET DEEP

short while and Freda along with her siblings remained behind to live with their grandparents. At the close of the evening she shared with me that this particular day was her birthday and when asked earlier that morning by her mother what she wanted for her birthday, her response was to meet me.

COVERING LIES

Freda and I dated for a while and later married. Within a year or two later, Byron (one of Janet's twins) graduated from a hair beauty salon school and decided to kick that up a notch with the interest of becoming a cosmetologist. He soon moved to California where he worked a short time in Hollywood as a make-up artist. He moved in with Janet's biological father Frank to scale back his cost of living expenses as well as assisting Frank in house chores and maintenance.

It could be attributed to an approaching Memorial Day holiday or simply a guilty conscience although Janet accepted in a laughing way in her sharing with Freda one day of a dream she had which caused her to wake up in the middle of the night. Throughout the lives of the Byron and Brett, she raised them with the belief that my grandfather Carl was the father of all three of us boys, he was a doctor, and died of cancer before they got to know him. On this particular night she dreamed that Byron went to the cemetery where Carl is to place flowers at the gravesite. She suddenly woke up in a panic realizing that if this ever really occurred, Byron would discover that Carl had been deceased eight years before his and Brett's births. To avoid being caught in that lie, the next morning she called the cemetery to have the marker on Carl's crypt which showed the date of his death removed.

When people start lying it seems they can't stop because they have to continue to cover each lie with another one. One lie leads to another, and there becomes a snowball effect to lying. It creates momentum so each one is easier to tell, until it catches up with a person. As a side

Fulfilling a Birthday Wish

note, I wonder what classification Janet and her lies fall under, after all, you may remember in her letter to me I was, "...just a cheap crook" because of all my "...lies and conning tactics."

TELL IT LIKE IT IS

I was always amazed that my new wife, Freda had an ability to express her opinions freely to Janet during discussions from time to time. The part that also amazed me was I could say something in either fact or disagreement to Janet and we'd fight like cats and dogs. Freda could say the exact thing and same tone of voice as I would, and Janet would either be speechless or understand and become in full agreement.

I'm not certain if it's a woman versus man or a woman versus woman chemistry aspect or what, but whatever it was it worked. I'm sure you women who are reading this now can provide the answers.

NEW ADDITION

We were blessed with our first child Clinton as Freda gave birth to him shortly before our third wedding anniversary. A few months later we bought a home in the small town of Skiatook which is located approximately twenty miles north of Tulsa. I turned a personal hobby into a business along with attending school for training to become a medic and firefighter, which allowed me to work part-time with the city ambulance department as well as a volunteer firefighter.

Clinton still has and occasionally talks about his memories from of all the times he got to ride in the firetruck with me during Pioneer Days and Christmas parades, turning on all the red flashing lights, and flipping the switch to make the siren change its various tones and sounds. Another memory he maintains is one which came a few years later. I was working the midnight shift as an ER Tech in a Tulsa hospital when Freda called to tell me she was going into labor with our daughter Tara. I called the ambulance to have her transported to the same hospital where I was working. During the trip to Tulsa, Clinton kept telling the ambulance driver to "Hurry up, my momma's having a baby!" and showed this driver where all the emergency light and siren switches were located and which ones to use.

LOST AND FOUND

During the year Freda became pregnant and throughout all of her pregnancy with Tara, we searched for my biological father and family. We made numerous trips to the Tulsa County Library and spent countless hours searching through multiple telephone directories of cities located in California, writing down all of those who shared my birthright last name, and their contact information. We'd take these lists of names home, and I would call every one of these people to inquire if they knew or heard of my father.

I was able to reach a woman who was my father's second cousin April, who knew of him but didn't know him directly. She was very knowledgable about our family heritage and sent me a copy of the pages from a family Bible with our family tree along with other information that she had gathered throughout the years. She also sent us a beautiful white laced dress as a gift for Tara after she was born, and Tara wore it during her baby dedication service at the church we attended.

Through April's genealogy records and information, I quickly learned that my paternal grandfather had two families at the same time. With his wife they had a daughter then a son, and with his mistress they also had a daughter then a son. The mother of my father and his sister Brenda was on the mistress side.

I also contacted my father's half brother Clifford, who was very delighted to meet me over the telephone and shared with me all the details of when, how, and where both he and my father met for the first

Fulfilling a Birthday Wish

and only time during their time serving in the military. We remained to correspond with each other for almost a year until he passed. I also contacted his older sister Marilyn, though she didn't receive me very well so I never made any more attempts to keep in contact with her.

FAVOR WITH HIGHER HELP

A young newly elected U.S. Congressman came to Skiatook for a Town Hall meeting, and we attended. We visited with him after the meeting and shared our desire, attempts, and difficulties in locating my father. He directed us to his assistant who also was at this meeting. We met with the assistant and was provided with many new leads and ideas to move forward in our search.

The following weekday morning I contacted the location where military records were stored, and was assisted by a very helpful man in the department I was connected to. He later mailed me some information I needed to assist in my search.

My second lead was with the Salvation Army who has a "Missing Persons" program. They provided me with forms to complete and other options to explore, however after several weeks and continued correspondence with them, their results came back empty handed.

The third lead was with an official U.S. government agency, in which there is a branch office in Tulsa. I went to the office, drew my number for a place in line, and waited. My number was called and I know it was the grace of God that I got to speak with a particular woman employee. I asked her a couple of curiosity questions that I had, and then shared with her what my search project was about, and provided the documentation that I received from the military records office and Salvation Army. She looked at her computer screen, made a couple of disappointing facial expressions, and then asked if I had ever tried contacting the Bureau of Vital Statistics office in California. I told her "no." Although I attempted without success, I hoped that maybe she had a different address to use. She excused herself to go to get the forms I needed, and in doing so it was almost like she intentionally put her hand on the computer screen as assistance to stand up because the screen monitor swiveled to where I could see it. Discretely I wrote down some information that I saw on display. When she returned, she pleasantly smiled and gave me the instructions to complete the form and mail it to the statistics office located in Sacramento.

I went home, completed the form, and placed it in the next days mail. Several weeks passed before I received a letter of response from the statistics office. Much to my sadness, the letter contained a certified copy of my father's death certificate. Freda and I got married, and he passed about a month later of the same year. Then we saw something that created another spark of hope. In the area marked as next of kin, my aunt Brenda's name was listed. I dialed "411" to hopefully get a telephone number, but there wasn't a listing for her and I couldn't recall her husband's first name.

Freda suggested that I go back to the government agency office to see what suggestions they may have. I did, and much my surprise (or favor of God) I got to speak to the very same woman who assisted me the first time. We both recognized each other and she remembered my reason for being there the first time. She asked if I had received any information from the statistics office and I showed her the death certificate. As she looked it over she started typing into her computer. She then looked up at me, smiled, and said she had an idea that could possibly help me. As she got up and excused herself momentarily, she used the same technique in using the computer monitor to assister in getting up. Again the monitor is turned and I have a view of the screen, and I discretely could see some certain information that I took note of just as I did for my father's information.

A few minutes later she returned and gave me the instructions to

Fulfilling a Birthday Wish

write two open letters: one to the agency explaining why I am looking for Aunt Brenda, and the second letter was to be addressed to her but not yet placed in a stamped envelope as so the agency can read the content of that letter as well. Then without any promise of results or response, the agency would forward my letter to Aunt Brenda. I immediately went home, wrote the letters (dated September 29, 1990), and returned them to the woman at the agency office.

The following week on Saturday evening October 6, 1990, we had just sat down at the table to eat supper when the telephone rang. Freda and I looked at each other with an expression that neither of us were expecting any calls, and then in hope that this was the call we were expecting. Indeed it was. Aunt Brenda had just received and read my letter. We cried, laughed, and cried more in rejoicing of our becoming reunited. She had so much to tell me and likewise I had so much to tell her. I realized after a while that we had been on the phone for an hour already, and I suggested that she give me her number so that we could hang up and then let me call her right back. This way we could split the cost of a long distance call, and we did. I immediately called her back and we talked for at least another hour.

THE TERM "KIDNAPPED"

Throughout our two plus hour telephone conversation, Aunt Brenda often referred to my being "kidnapped." I had never heard that expression as my being taken from California by Janet, because it had always been my understanding that my father had given Janet permission to do so. However, Aunt Brenda was very adamant in her using the term kidnapped. She told me that even my father came to Oklahoma to help the law enforcement search for me but had run into dead ends with his searches as well as out of money.

I made a simple comment about when Janet "put me away," and Aunt Brenda questioned me about that statement. "What do you mean Janet put you away?" When I explained to her about Janet sending me to the children's and boys homes Aunt Brenda almost became furious. She then told me all of my family in California thought that I was probably living a comfortable and happy life, not knowing I had lived in my own private hell, and to hear that I was placed in these homes was shattering to her. I never told her about the other problems I experienced growing up as mentioned earlier this book, because I know it would have really crushed her heart.

The following week I received a letter that was seven and a half pages long and it took her a few days to write it. We continued to write each other and in lengthy letters we were able to exchange a lot of information.

NOTES:

Chapter 14
Reunion Plans

Within a couple of weeks after our contact with Aunt Brenda, we also got to talk to her oldest daughter Patty. She is a year and a half older than me, and although we are cousins, we were almost like brother and sister when we were little children.

The following month and a half was a very eventful time for us. We sold our home, put a contract on another one in Tulsa, enjoyed the Thanksgiving holiday, packed our belongings, closed on both homes on the same day, interviewed for a new job, moved, unpacked, decorated the new home with Christmas decorations, completed our Christmas shopping, enjoyed Christmas in our new home, and was called the day after to be informed that I was being offered that position for the job I interviewed for.

For the next several months we made plans and saved up for a three week vacation to go to California and reunite with Aunt Brenda, Uncle Mack and my cousins. Along with our meeting up with them, April began planning for a family reunion as well, because this was going to be the first time that it would include both the married and mistress sides of our family to ever be together.

We also wanted to include the chance visit with Doris, Lewis, Bonita, and Dan during this trip as well. They moved to California several years earlier due to Lewis' employer transferring him from Tulsa to the northern part of California. Dan visited a few times when passing through or near Tulsa with his job from time to time, and in doing so stayed with his father Duane and of course Janet. Bonita didn't have that opportunity to travel or visit as much like her brother did.

LET THE GOOD TIMES ROLL

The day arrived that when I got off work at six o'clock, I rushed home, changed clothes, and we hit the road as we were now on vacation time and California bound. Freda used that day to pack our clothes and load the baggage in the car, as well as prepared sandwiches, chips, fruits, and drinks to eat while on the road.

We arrived at Aunt Brenda's a couple of days later. This was the first time of our getting to see each other in thirty-four years. We cried, we hugged, and we cried some more. It almost seemed at times like it was a dream and hard to imagine that it wasn't, and if it was I didn't want to wake up. I'm so thankful it wasn't a dream at all.

The first couple of days there were spent just visiting with Uncle Mac and Aunt Brenda and trying to catch up on lost time. My cousins Patty and Jenna arrived to join in on our festivity as well, and of course this was the first time I'd seen Patty since I was six years old, and the first time ever of getting to meet Jenna.

The only difficult time I had emotionally was when Aunt Brenda handed me a box that contained some personal items that belonged to my father. However, what a surprise it was within that box, to discover and see all the baby pictures he had of me. I didn't even know any of my baby pictures even existed. What a treat!

One picture in particular that stood out later that I found very interesting. We are guessing my age to be around three years old, and I'm with my father standing in front of the Yuma Territorial Prison in Yuma, Arizona. At the time I first saw this picture it didn't have the

Reunion Plans

meaning to me as it does now because of the area of ministry that I've been involved in for the past several years. God knew then of His plans for me to be in the prison ministry, and now I have a picture being at my first prison at the age of three.

This is another example of the fulfillment in His Word as shown in Scripture, "For I know the plans I have for you, says the Lord. They are plans for good and not for disaster, to give you a future and a hope." (Jeremiah 29:11 NLT)

We launched out for some days of entertainment with meeting April and spending the day with her going to Disneyland. We took other days to go to Long Beach to see the Queen Mary, the beaches, nearby parks in the evenings, and shopping malls.

COMING TOGETHER

April's reunion plan was a huge success. I don't know the number of hours she spent in putting this together, but she did an awesome job of sending out letters and invitations, making phone calls, placing the reservations at a large park, preparing menus, and cooking. The final count including children was seventy-eight family members from all across the state of California, as well as from Colorado and Utah were in attendance to this grand reunion occasion, and having us to be known as the guests of honor. What a blessing this was, and a trip worth making to my home state.

CONFIRMATION

It's amazing how time flies when you're having fun. We had been in California for nearly two weeks and it was almost time to start making our trip back home. Before we could, we needed to make a days trip northward to visit with Doris and Lewis.

SIX FEET DEEP

These 2 photos were taken (Then)
at Yuma Territorial Prison in Yuma, Arizona.

"For I know the plans I have for you, says the Lord....

Here with my father at the Yuma Territorial Prison

Reunion Plans

These 2 photos were taken (Now)
at Yuma Territorial Prison in Yuma, Arizona.

...They are plans for good and not for disaster, to give you a future and a hope." (Jeremiah 29:11 NLT)

A time of reflection while revisiting Yuma Territorial Prison

SIX FEET DEEP

We left early in the morning and arrived at Doris and Lewis' home during the early afternoon. She had prepared a wonderful fruit and sandwich brunch for us, and as we visited and ate, Clinton and Tara made use of the swimming pool under Bonita's supervision. We missed getting to see Dan as he was in Alaska on a job sight.

I don't recall how the conversation got started, but Doris made the comment, "Oh Stevie, I've always so wished that you could have found your real family." Freda and I just looked at each other but didn't say anything. We continued listening to Doris' conversation, in which most of it was about Janet and Doris' dislike for her. Then she popped the comment, "There's just so many skeletons in the closet." Then I softly said, "Yeah, I bet I can name a few." "What was that dear?" she asked. Not realizing I had initially said it loud enough for her to hear me, I repeated, "Oh I just said that I could probably name some of those skeletons." "Well, of course you can. You know you were kidnapped don't you?" I just about choked over the bite I was about to swallow. I asked, "What did you say?" She said, "You do know you were kidnapped. Right? Why else do you think Janet always hid you out in mine and Duane's house every time she left Oklahoma to come here to California? The law enforcement was looking to take you back."

Realizing she was being very sincere and truthful, I finally spoke out and told her, "Well Doris, I don't want to hurt your feelings in any way, but, you're not the only reason we came to California." She answered back, "Oh I know dear, you all have been on a wonderful vacation, taking the kids to Disneyland and all over. We weren't expecting you to come here just for us." Then I let it out, "To be honest with you, I found my family last year, and we've just spent the last two weeks with them." The moment I said that, she quickly turned around, her mouth dropped open, an expression of joy appeared on her face, and her eyes filled with tears. "Oh I am so happy for you!"

We continued our conversation along with reminiscing of old things of the past that occurred when I stayed with her and Duane when I was a small child. Lewis arrived home and we filled him in on all what we had discussed. Freda and I were utterly amazed how Doris' knowledge and comments were almost identical in content and descriptive as that of what Aunt Brenda had told us. Two totally different women who never met or knew each other, yet exactly the same knowledge and stories.

Our spending time there with them was only until the following morning, but it was a very refreshing time. We appreciated the emotional support that we received from the Lewis, Doris, and Bonita. This was an example of what true family, friends, and relationships are all about. We left their home with one more destination left in our plans before our return trip for home and our arrival into the San Diego area was early that evening. The next day we spent the entire time enjoying all the attractions and events offered at Sea World, and began our return trip to home the following morning.

PROOF IN THE PUDDING

Our two day road trip for returning home allowed my mind to ponder on many thoughts as well as many discussions with Freda. With the way my schedule was set at work, I would be on duty for two days, off for two days, work for three days, and off for two days. I created a plan to visit the courthouse for my first day off once we got home, back to work, and back into the normal swing of things.

As planned for my first day off I went to the county courthouse and visited the Records Division. When asked by the clerk if she could help me, I told her that I'd like to view my adoption records and provided her the information she requested from me. She returned a few minutes later and apologized that she couldn't let me have access to these records because they sealed. I asked her out of curiosity, "How does a person get records unsealed?" She explained this had to be done through the order of a judge. I then asked her if she could provide me with a name of any judges, and she did.

When I asked if the judge was located within the same building, she confirmed that he was and gave me the room number. I left and went to the judges office, briefly spoke with his secretary to see if he was available, and she introduced me to Judge W.

Judge W and I exchanged our introduction comments and he asked me how he could help me. "Well, Sir I'm a forty year old man, I know that I'm adopted, and both of my parents are deceased." He looked at me with a little bit of a puzzling expression on his face and asked, "So exactly what is it you need from me?" I then said, "I wanted to view my adoption records and the woman downstairs wouldn't let me because she said they were sealed and that I needed a judge's order to have them unsealed. Then she gave me your name, so here I am to see what needs to be done." "Is that all you need?" he asked. He then called out to his secretary to have her call downstairs with his order to unseal my adoption records. "Anything else?" he asked. "No Sir" I replied. We shook hands and I was on my way back downstairs.

The clerk met me at the counter and handed me the file. With pen and pad in one hand and the file in the other, I sat down to search a history of my life and take notes. It wasn't long before I couldn't write fast enough to contain all the information I was discovering. Part of it may be true, but then I found one lie for sure. I don't claim to be or have the full knowledge of a medical doctor, however, as a former paramedic I do have enough education and training in the medical field to know that if a person has a scar from either a bad burn or cut, that scar will remain with that person for the remainder of his or her life. According to these legal documents which were filed in a county court, it states that when I was an infant I was placed in scalding hot water, and that I still had the scars around my genital area from the burns. I went ahead to have a physical examination from a doctor and there are no scars.

Reunion Plans

Next I found an item that really caught my attention which answered longing questions that I had for a number of years - Did my father really give his consent to Janet; and if not, how did she legally adopt me without his consent? This item was a copy of a receipt and a small yellow / ivory colored piece of paper, which was a classified ad published in the Tulsa Legal News that stated "NOTICE OF APPLICATION FOR ADOPTION WITHOUT CONSENT OF PARENT AND HEARING."

It continued to address this matter to my father and Janet's intent to adopt me on the grounds my natural mother was deceased and ruled by the courts in Los Angeles that I was deprived of the custody and experienced cruelty and neglect by my natural father. Therefore, my father was being informed of the hearing being set in nineteen days, and advised, "...you must appear and defend against said application or thereafter be forever barred." I believe its rather hard for a man in the Los Angeles area to read a paper that's normally only read by lawyers, and printed for those in Tulsa.

My first thought after reading this was, "I've got to have a copy of this." I immediately went to the clerk and asked her if she would make me a copy. "No, I'm sorry. The judge didn't say anything about making copies. He only said you could view the record." I told her to hold onto to the file, as I'd be right back. I then rushed back up to the judges office and told his secretary there was a problem. She nodded her head in motioning that I could see him. As I entered into his chamber, he was zipping up his black robe in preparation to enter the courtroom. "Make it quick" he said, "I'm due on docket momentarily." I repeated to him what the woman clerk said about my not being allowed to have copies. His initial politeness in personality suddenly changed as he harshly and loudly spoke out to his secretary, "Call down there and tell that (blankety blank) to give this young man anything he wants!" He then turned his head, looked at me, smiled, and said, "You shouldn't have anymore problems."

101

SIX FEET DEEP

I'm not sure exactly what or how the secretary relayed the judge's instructions, but the clerk was no longer as pleasant with me as she had been earlier. "Just exactly what is it you want a copy of?" she asked in frustration. "Well, ma'am, I believe I want a copy of the whole file." I replied back. "You know that's going to take me some time!" I answered her saying, "Yes I'm sure it will. I have the rest of the day free." "I'll have to charge you for the copies!" she continued to snap. "I have some money with me." I said assuringly.

Within approximately thirty minutes she was finished with making the copies, I paid her, wished her a good day, and walked out with my prize possession of the evidence that demonstrates the truth.

NOTES:

Chapter 15
Hidden in the Dirt

We spent the next several days reviewing the content of my adoption records, and shocked in the discovery of what was said and filed. In my telling Aunt Brenda what I was reading, she too was shocked and in disbelief with all the lies these legal documents contained. To assure myself against any loss or damage to these important documents, I made an additional copy of the full record and mailed it to my cousin Patty for her safe keeping as well.

I contacted the courts and law offices in California that were listed in the documents and I quickly learned that some of the same people involved in this matter were still practicing law, including the District Attorney. I spoke with him on numerous occasions with questions that I had, and he was very helpful in providing the information I needed. This included my finding out that the warrant issued for Janet's arrest was still in effect. Now a couple of things are beginning to add up. First, I remembered back when Janet and I first came to Oklahoma, as well as our short stay in California during my junior year in high school, regarding her fear of the multiples times that someone was following her and the attempts to lose those possibly doing so. Secondly I recall when Byron was living in California and staying with Janet's father. Frank became ill and never recovered from it. After his passing away, Janet made it very clear that Byron was to be the executor of the estate, handle all the burial arrangements, the sale of Frank's home and property, moving all of Frank's personal belongings, furniture, etc., to Tulsa and for her name to never be mentioned or appear in any of the documentations.

SIX FEET DEEP
CALL OF DUTY

I received a summons to appear at the Tulsa County Courthouse for jury duty selection. At the break time for lunch, another prospective juror asked if he could join me at the table where I sat, and I accepted. After our introduction of names, I asked him what his work profession was. He told me that he was a psychologist and worked as a counselor at the Tulsa Boys' Home. "Really!" I exclaimed, and then told him that I lived at their old location when I was younger. After he asked questions about my past, and my telling him of my life's story, he said, "Wow, in all reality you should have been in a prison somewhere because most boys with a background like yours end up spending most of their lives in prison. You have really beaten the odds and I commend you."

MORE LOST AND FOUND

Freda and Janet often went out for lunch and shopping in the mall. On one such occasion Freda broke the news to Janet that I had found my family and our vacation to California was spent with those family members. To our surprise, Janet accepted this news very well and appeared happy for us. However, she again was very adamant in her warning that I wasn't to ever try to contact anyone from the Young side of the family. Her reasoning behind this, as I had heard this all my life as well, was because the "Young's were untrustworthy people, and that I would hear many lies about her," and my life.

It was interesting and very timely that this conversation took place because in reviewing my adoption records I had also begun a search for my mother's brother, Uncle Glen. Our world of technology was beginning to develop with the use of computers and communications were made through search engines and bulletin boards. I used the resources that were available to me but still ran into a dead end.

My knowing the requirements of the government agency gave me

Hidden in the Dirt

when I was looking for Aunt Brenda became refreshed in my mind, and I began writing the two letters they would ask for. I arrived at the agency, took a number, and sat down until my number was called just like in the past. There's no way to explain this because I don't believe in coincidence, although I do believe in divine appointment. When I went to the desk of the clerk who called my number, it was same woman who helped me the two previous times. I told her about my desire to locate Uncle Glen, gave her the two open letters, and shared with her some of the stories from our vacation reunion trip that we took earlier that summer. I again thanked her for all of her assistance and left.

On the evening following Thanksgiving, Freda answered the telephone and heard a man's voice ask, "Is this the Young's residence?" She confirmed that it was and he introduced himself as "Steve's Uncle Glen." She immediately gave me the phone and our holiday weekend had just become complete. I was a little nervous at first but quickly became relaxed as I could tell in his sincerity of his voice and comments that I was being accepted and welcomed into his family. I can't explain in words the feeling of completeness and acceptance that I experienced that evening. The last of the missing piece of the puzzle in my life was now found, and the picture made complete.

Almost immediately we started corresponding with letters as I continued to load him down with questions. Two very interesting pieces of his information became very clear to me: The first involved Ralph the brick mason and so called father of Byron and Brett. When Ralph and Janet were together, he began learning of the legal issues of my grandfather Carl's estate and my adoption. He called Uncle Glen on a couple of occasions, and mentioned that he was being pulled into a trap of some kind. Then when Janet became pregnant, Ralph told Uncle Glen in their last telephone conversation, that he wasn't the father because he was sterile. There had been years of speculation that before Janet's mother Aubrey and stepfather Greg moved from California to Tulsa, there had been some inappropriate relationships that occurred between

Janet and Greg. The second piece of information referred to the time shortly after Janet and Duane got married and the evening I broke the cardinal rule of going to the convenience store with my two neighbors. Apparently in Janet's attempts to have me made a ward of the court backfired because of my age, so she contacted Uncle Glen in asking him if he would take me into his household. Hmmmm, I remember her saying, "don't contact the Young side of the family because the Young's were untrustworthy people, and I would hear many lies about her." Her own words were beginning to trap her.

NOTES:

Chapter 16
Maturity

Throughout the time beginning from my and Freda's marriage our relationship with Janet and Duane had reached a level of being smoothed out with little or no conflict. Duane was always the quiet one, possibly because of Janet's demanding and domineering personality, along with her manipulating mannerisms, there wasn't any issues that caused him and I to ever have any problems. I purposely avoided allowing any conflict between me and Janet. To help maintain peace in the family, it was never revealed to Janet that we contacted Uncle Glen and continued to correspond with him as well as with Aunt Brenda and her family.

ANOTHER OUTBURST

One weekend morning when Clinton was at the age of eleven or twelve years old, Janet came to our home unannounced. I saw a familiar facial expression she had and instead of greeting us with any pleasantness, she stated that she wanted to talk with Clinton alone in her car. We had no idea what was up or why she wanted to talk with him. After an approximate of fifteen to twenty minutes passed, he came in as she drove off. Clinton appeared to have been crying and was emotionally upset. When asked what happened, he explained that she had accused him of stealing one of her cheap cubic zirconia rings and told him he was "A thief and I no longer know you." This is again is an example of the trait about her. If someone crosses her, she accuses them and disowns them. We've seen long and short term friendships end because of this, she's done it to me, and now she did it to our son.

SIX FEET DEEP

I waited to allow Janet enough time to get home before calling her. The stone, and not a ring, that Clinton had was one he found on the sidewalk at a shopping center a few evenings before when she took Clinton and Tara to. We argued and raised our voices until she hung up on me.

Several months had passed and our daughter Tara continued to express comments of sadness in missing her grandpa. For whatever the reason, I broke the silence of communications and called Janet. I could tell by the tone in her voice that she was startled after hearing my voice when she answered the telephone. Slowly over a short time, the relationship and contact again mended.

TIME OF FORGIVENESS

Another year or two passed when one evening we were at Janet and Duane's house. Without any forethoughts, intentions, or plans to do so I unexpectedly and somewhat blurted out to Janet that throughout my life that I had developed feelings of hatred, bitterness, as well as call her names, cursed her behind her back. I then offered my apology and asked her to forgive me for all of those areas. Her facial expressed her being shocked and momentarily she was speechless. She then expressed her acceptance of my apology and willingness to forgive, even with a tone in her voice of being dismayed. That particular conversation quickly ended and we visited a little longer before leaving for home.

Almost immediately after getting into our car to leave, Freda looked at me and said, "I can't believe what you just did and said to Janet." In shock myself, I replied back, "I can't either. It just came out of me, and I don't know who was the most shocked out of it all, me or her, but I feel good about it."

As I reflect upon that moment, I believe it was the grace of God that enabled me to ask for forgiveness. Even though there was no

Maturity

reciprocation of Janet asking for forgiveness. I know I did what God wanted me to do period. I knew then I was released in spirit. I also knew that i was no longer under Janet's control. I was free inside.

FINAL BATTLE

Less than six months later, there was a misunderstanding between us and Janet's son Byron which later led into a civil court matter. The day before the court date and during a telephone conversation with Janet and Freda, Janet detected that Freda sounded a little depressed and asked if things were okay. Freda stated that she was a little upset and nervous regarding the upcoming court matter. Janet told her "not to be worried about it" and "things will all work out."

The following day we arrived at the courtroom a little early and had Clinton with us. Just before the court session was to begin, Byron came in with Janet at his side. The judge heard both sides of our case, and at the close of our explanations, Janet stood up, introduced herself, and asked the judge if she could briefly make a comment. In his allowance of her to do so, she spoke in defense of Byron's behalf and presented only half of the truth in the matter.

The judge ruled in Byron's behalf after listening to Janet's fictional story, and instructed us to make some payment arrangements with Byron for the amount awarded. As Janet and Byron began exiting the courtroom and passing Clinton, he noticed the facial expression that Janet had, compared to that of a proud hen, and heard her softly say to Byron, "We did it."

Two weeks later when I received my paycheck from my employer, I noticed it to be lower than usual. I contacted the personnel department to learn that Byron had filed a garnishment against my income. We went back to court were blessed to have the same judge. He verbally reprimanded Byron for filing the garnishment and ordered him to refund the amount that was deducted from my check. Byron personally and purposely didn't give us the refund, as it was later added back to my paycheck because the check issued to him through the initial garnishment was never cashed, and the required time to do so lapsed.

By our choice it's been over a decade since we broke off our relationship and contact with Janet and her family. As the result, we haven't and don't miss the immaturity, trivial drama, and endless lies in the world in which they live in.

NOTES:

Chapter 17
Lies

As I shared in a previous chapter, when people start lying it seems they can't stop because they have to continue to cover each lie with another one. One lie leads to another, then another, to another, until there becomes a snowball effect to lying and it creates a momentum so each lie is easier to tell. Lies remind me of chapters in a book. When one lie (or a chapter) ends, another lie (chapter) begins. At some point the chapters in a book end, and it's important in a person's life that lies need to end as well.

Lies also create a sense of fear in that the liar become afraid he or she will get caught and therefore continues to create more lies for a cover up of the ones already told. These lies and fears are not of or from God, but originates from the devil himself. Scripture tells us,"...there is no truth in him. When he speaks a lie, he speaks from his own resources, for he is a liar and the father of it." (John 8:44 NKJV)

Lies destroy lives! They not only destroy, they often hurt, damage, penetrate and pierce the hearts of those who were lied to or about, but they also destroy the character, personality, and reputation of the habitual liar themselves. This is the same characteristic as the enemy referred to in John 10:10, "The thief does not come except to steal, kill, and destroy." Thankfully Jesus came that we, "...may have life, and have it more abundantly."

Lying cannot truly be the character of person of honesty and speak lies at the same time. The liar cannot live a life of truth with the Lord, and serve a life of lies for the devil.

Lies are a deceptive way of life, proving the liar cannot and is not a trustworthy person. The lies are made with a deliberate intent to deceive the truth and create harm to others with verbal attacks of assault.

It's interesting that a liar has no memory. They cannot remember from one lie to another to cover what they told in the past. This is seen almost daily within the legal systems around the world during court proceedings. The defendants repeatedly use one lie to cover another. As a result the liar continues a pattern of telling more lies from the ones already told using more lies to cover old lies with new lies. Do you see a common word in that last sentence? The liar's world is surrounded and entangled with that one single word -"lies".

Lies have no color or measure. There is no such thing as "a little white lie" or a "half-truth" or a "half-lie". This is like saying a light switch is either "on" or "off". This is impossible! It's either "on" or it's "off". Likewise, a lie is a lie, and there is no truth in them period.

QUOTES ABOUT LIES

"If you tell the truth, you don't have to remember anything."
- Mark Twain

"I'm not upset that you lied to me, I'm upset that from now on I can't believe you." - Friedrich Nietzsche

"Lies and secrets, they are like a cancer in the soul. They eat away what is good and leaves only destruction behind."
- Cassandra Clare, Clockwork Prince

"A lie that is half-truth is the darkest of all lies." - Alfred Tennyson

Lies

Above all, don't lie to yourself. The man who lies to himself and listens to his own lies comes to a point he cannot distinguish the truth within him, or around him, and so loses all respect for himself and for others. And having no respect he ceases to love."

- Fyodor Dostoyevsky, The Brothers Karamazov

"Watch your thoughts;
they become words.
Watch your words;
they become actions.
Watch your actions;
they become habits.
Watch your habits;
they become character.
Watch your character;
it becomes your destiny."

- Unknown

THE ULTIMATE GOAL

It's easy for us to lash out or retaliate when we've been hurt and is difficult to just let it go. Walking away from injustices often seems wrong although it's often the correct way to go. There comes a time in our life when we must surrender, not necessarily to the injustice, not to the hurt, not to the past, but to the leading of God and His Spirit of mercy and power making our life stronger than the injustice. It is the Lord who heals the broken hearted and binds up our wounds. (Psalm 147:3)

The Lord will also work in our behalf regarding other people. There are times when the Holy Spirit will direct a person who has experienced injustice to go to others who can help correct what needs to be corrected in order to stop someone from hurting more people. You can know through prayer what God's leading will be in matters. Whatever is done will not be from a wrong motive when you are being led by The Lord.

SIX FEET DEEP

Forgiveness is not about forgetting, as that would lead to denial, but it is about letting go of the past and not dwelling on the hurt caused by the other person. Forgiveness doesn't mean you have to embrace or keep a relationship with that person who hurt you either. When someone has not yet shown evidence of being changed, it creates a lack of trust. Sometimes it is better to sever the ties of a relationship with those who have severely hurt us emotionally, physically, or mindfully. Even Jesus knew that someone could not be trusted, "Jesus didn't trust them, because He knew human nature. No one needed to tell Him what mankind is really like." (John 2:24, 25 NLT) Until a person has shown evidence of change, we forgive but we go forward in another direction. When you become a Christian, and I'm not talking about practicing religion, but surrendering your life to Christ, you transform your old man (old life and ways) to one that is a new character, a new love, a new spirit within you, a new sense of peace, and a new sense of forgiveness. Paul tells us in Colossians 3:12-13, "Since God chose you to be the holy people whom He loves, you must clothe yourselves with tenderhearted mercy, kindness, humility, gentleness, and patience. You must make allowance for each other's faults and forgive the person who offends you. Remember, the Lord forgave you, so you must forgive others." (NLT)

So what is forgiveness? Sometimes when we choose to forgive, the other person doesn't have an understanding spiritually to want reconciliation or don't respond in a reconciling manner. Forgiveness then has to be a faith step on our part. We choose to forgive because Christ's love inside us, "Do not let the evil defeat you, but defeat evil by doing good." (Romans 12:21) Forgiveness is made possible through Christ who forgave us (Luke 23:34; Col. 1:14). It's an act in which one person releases another from an offense, refusing to enact the penalty due him or her, refusing to sustain consideration of the cause of the offense, and refusing to allow that offense to affect the relationship. Such forgiveness releases one from a sense of unresolved guilt, restores a clear conscience, and restores relationship. To forgive is not to condone the sin as acceptable, to say it made no difference, or to license repetition of it. Rather, forgiveness is a choice. It's a decision made to no longer hold an offense against another person or group. It restores the person you are forgiving to the same position they had before, as if what they did never happened. If possible save your relationships and be quick to forgive. Someday, you too will need forgiveness.

The greatest power you have over anyone who has hurt you is the power of forgiveness. When you say, "I forgive you," you in essence are saying, "I no longer hold it against you." Both you and that other person are set free from the negative bond that existed between you. It also frees you from no longer being the offended person, and you no longer call them the offender. You become known as the forgiver, and they become known as the forgiven.

I think of the excruciating pain that Jesus experienced the day of His crucifixion. As they drove those nails through His hands and feet, although He yelled out due to physical pain He never yelled back, didn't curse at them, no bitterness or hatred remarks toward them ever came out of His mouth, no thoughts of retaliation, instead He said, "Father, forgive them; for they know not what they do." (Luke 23:34)

One of our great weaknesses and temptations is to hold on to anger or grudges toward our enemies. Forgiveness not only liberates the other person, but it also liberates you. It really is the way to true freedom. I know personally that forgiving doesn't always mean forgetting. As told in this book, my memories of all the physical pain, emotional pain, mental anguish, abuse, abandonment, distrust, violations, and hatred that I experienced has stayed with me my entire life. However, the forgiveness that I offered several years ago, changes the way I remember it all. Throughout the writing of this book, I had to relive all the feelings and experiences that I had, and purposely wrote those thoughts as I had them then. Through God's grace I now have a whole new outlook on these experiences, as I don't look at them in cursing way but instead as a blessing, with the hope if I can succeed into successfully ministering to one person and having him or her to surrender their hate and unforgiveness into forgiveness, I've accomplished my goal.

NOTES:

Chapter 18
Instruction on Forgiveness

One morning I heard from the Lord saying, "Be careful, that chip on your shoulder can be heavier than you think." Scripture instructs, "...let us strip off every weight that slows us down, especially the sin that so easily hinders our progress." (Hebrews 12:1 NLT) The sins of bitterness, anger, hate, and unforgiveness will and does weigh us down if we don't let go of them and replace them with love and forgiveness. We see and hear of this almost daily the news of killings and it is growing every day. People aren't killing other people just to be doing it. Anger is the root of these killings. As it develops the weight of thoughts are added, then dwelled on, and crimes are committed. The person with the anger issue may not kill the other person physically, but they can and do so mentally to the other person. How many families have become estranged because of verbal assault, hate, jealousy, physical assault or violation, and anger? More importantly, how many of these family members remain unforgiving toward one another? There are countless men and women who have been hurt from the experience from their marriage which ended in divorce, and continue to hold those feelings of anger, bitterness, distrust, and unforgiveness. They also continue to blame their ex-spouse for their own misery, inferiority, and lack of self respect. There are numerous mothers and fathers suffering from being brokenhearted because of the bitterness that their son(s) or daughter(s) had when he or she stomped out of the home full of anger. There are numerous siblings that are heartbroken because of resentment where it appeared the other obtained more favor and provisions while growing up. There are numerous adults who are incarcerated and maintain hatred and bitterness toward their parents because their parents wouldn't or didn't bail them out of jail, or who have literally disowned them because of their incarceration status. It's time to forgive! We all make mistakes, all of us have sinned (Romans 3:23), and we all need to do is repent, forgive, ask for forgiveness, and get over it!

An area of instruction given to me to study from the Lord were these three Scriptures: 1) Jesus tells us in Matthew 5:43-44, "You have heard that it was said, 'You shall love our neighbor and hate your enemy.' But I say to you, love your enemies, bless those who curse you, do good to those who hate you, and pray for those who spitefully use you and persecute you." 2) In His teaching us how to pray to our Father, Jesus clearly instructs us to, "...forgive us our sins, just as we have forgiven those who have sinned against us." (Matthew 6:12 NLT); and 3) "But when you are praying, first forgive anyone you are holding a grudge against, so that your Father in heaven will forgive your sins, too." (Mark 11:25 NLT) I know personally through my life's experiences, for a very long time I maintained an attitude, "I'm not the one at fault. I'm the adopted child, I'm the victim. I'm not the one who inflicted the physical and mental wounds and scars, and therefore, before I do any forgiving Janet must come forward first, and then I'll think about it." Then, after my listening to the Lord, reading His Word, I realized two things: First, I was wrong in my thinking and reasoning; and second, that is not what Scripture says. It says I am to love my enemies, those who spitefully used and persecuted me; I am to forgive those who sinned against me; and I am to forgive those who I have held a grudge against. Scripture does not say to wait for the other person to make the first move or to take the first step toward reconciliation. It just doesn't inform us, but it instructs us to do these efforts. Forget the pity party and trying to reason out who is at fault. Forgive, forget, and move forward! Move forward with the life the Lord has planned for you, and in the blessings He wishes to provide for you. I would not be experiencing the abundance of blessings and in the area of ministry that I am today, IF I wouldn't have asked for forgiveness from Janet that one evening at her home. If I

Instruction on Forgiveness

hadn't offered my apology and asked for forgiveness when I did before having that final dispute between Janet and me, I most likely would still be living with those weights of sin in my life, and be struggling within my personal life as well as in the ministry the Lord has called me to do.

For most of us, the decision to forgive is difficult and straightforward. We first choose to fogive by faith. Since the spirit of faith is "I believe and therefore I speak" (II Cor. 4:13), we first speak in prayer, "I choose to forgive (<u>NAME OF PERSON</u>) in Jesus' Name. Lord I know you have forgiven me of my sins so I choose to forgive (<u>NAME OF PERSON</u>) because of your love within me. Forgiveness is a journey that requires time, perseverance, prayer, and effort. It is something that is seldom easy, but is always right. When we forgive those who have hurt us, we are honoring God by our obedience of His commandments. One of the best ways to forgive someone is to begin praying for them. Then pray for yourself by asking the Lord to heal your heart, your hurts, to mend your emotions, and bind your bitterness.

Believe when you pray that you receive His healing within your heart and soul. That's faith! Faith believes to receive the moment we pray. (Mark 11:24) Then begin thanking God for His healing within your life. Worship also brings healing because you get your focus on God instead of yourself. There is healing in worshipping God. Also begin to read and meditate God's Word. His Word brings healing to our souls and comfort that is supernatural. He begins to fill us with His love and grace.

LOVE

Jesus said that one characteristic that people will be able to know that we are His disciples is that we have love for one another (John 13:35). Disciples of Jesus know and understand that His love within our hearts to love others even in difficult times and circumstances is not always easy. Thankfully it's through the Lord's grace and power that helps us to love others regardless of our feelings of hurt, betrayal, bitterness, etc., because our ability to love is not based on our own human efforts or feelings.

His love and grace will begin to open our hearts to demonstrate kindness to others. Most people who have been abused have not known this aspect of life. The Holy Spirit will begin to awaken you to this attribute. The scripture says, "In everything treat others as you would want then to treat you." (Matt. 7:12 NET) Proverbs 11:17 says, "Your kindness will reward you, but your cruelty will destroy you." (NLT) Kindness is a choice. Most of us find it easy to be kind when we feel happy and generous. However, the commandment that God gave us is not based on our feelings. He intends for us to treat each other with kindness and respect, regardless of circumstances.

Forgiveness, love, and kindness are attributes of our Christian faith. We are to daily remind ourselves of this. To help clarify and remind us of this, I love this set of instructions given to us by the Apostle Paul, "Get rid of all bitterness, rage, anger, harsh words, and slander, as well as all types of evil behavior. Instead, be kind to each other, tenderhearted, forgiving one another, just as God through Christ has forgiven you." (Ephesians 4:31-32) NLT

Here are helpful ways to express these attributes:
- Listen without Interrupting   Proverbs 18:13
- Speak without Accusing   James 1:19
- Give without Sparing   Proverbs 21:26
- Pray without Ceasing   Colossians 1:9
- Answer without Arguing   Proverbs 17:1
- Enjoy without Complaining   Philippians 2:14
- Trust without Wavering   1 Cor. 13:7
- Forgive without Punishing   Colossians 3:13

Instruction on Forgiveness
COLLECTION OF CLICHE'S AND QUOTES

While in Rwanda, Africa during June 2008 for a summer crusade along with Pastor D and his wife, we were eating lunch together one day. I really don't recall how the subject started, but in our discussion I mentioned to them that I entertained the thought of writing a book which would share my biography along with the focus and provision of Biblical principles on forgiveness. Pastor D told me I must write the book, even though I down played it because I thought it would be self centered. He corrected my thinking as he told me that I'd be sharing in my testimony, the same things that others may have or are experiencing in their lives as well. He told me I must make this writing, and if I did he would write the forward for me.

After our return from Rwanda, my ministry schedule became full with other trips, holidays, establishing our Bible college within more prisons, etc. I procrastinated in my writing. In November 2009, my pastor experienced the ultimate graduation by leaving this earth and into his eternal home in heaven with our Lord. As a result from this, his leaving knocked the wind out from underneath my sails in writing this book. Although I wanted to write it, the thoughts of his willingness to assist me with his words to be written in the forward would no longer be an option, and I would lose my interest in it by setting my notes aside. Then one late afternoon while driving on the highway, the Lord spoke and informed me that my focus on the book was off target. Instead of looking to Him for the content to be written and the ability to minister to those who need this message, I was focussed on promotion and words in the forward that Pastor D would have been led to write. The Lord then instructed me to set the old thoughts and focus aside, focus on Him and His direction, and complete this book.

I'm including the following list of statements and quotes that I've collected over the past four years regarding thoughts on forgiveness:

SIX FEET DEEP

- A friend of mine who is also a contemporary Christian recording artist sent me this,
   > "The first to apologize is the bravest.
   > The first to forgive is the strongest.
   > The first to forget is the happiest."

- "Forgiveness is not about forgetting. It is about letting go of another person's throat...Forgiveness does not create a relationship. Unless people speak the truth about what they have done and change their mind and behavior, a relationship of trust is not possible. When you forgive someone you certainly release them from judgement, but without true change, no real relationship can be established. Forgiveness in no way requires that you trust the one you forgive. But should they finally confess and repent, you will discover a miracle in your own heart that allows you to reach out and begin to build between you a bridge of reconciliation. Forgiveness does not excuse anything. You may have to declare your forgiveness a hundred times the first day and the second day, but the third day will be less and each day after, until one day you will realize that you have forgotten completely. And then one day you will pray for His wholeness..."
   - Wm. Paul Young, The Shack

- "Hatred stirs up strife, but love covers all sin." - Proverbs 10:12

- "Holding a grudge is letting someone live rent free in you head"

- "Your walk talks and your talk walks. But your walk talks louder than your talk"

- "Love prospers when a fault is forgiven, but dwelling on it separates close friends." - Proverbs 17:9 NLT

- "What you don't forgive you become. Don't become what it is

Instruction on Forgiveness

that you hate."

• "If you can see the invisible, God can do the impossible."

• "There's a few problems with unforgiveness: it's sneaky, contagious, and lethal."

• Life is too short...love the people who treat you right, and forgive the ones who don't."

• No matter where you have been, no matter what you have said, no matter what you have done, Jesus forgives. He waits for you with open arms.

• Forgiveness...it's not about the person that has hurt you, its if you don't forgive, it will hold you (not them) into bondage. It will kill you from the inside out. Remember, the Bible says to forgive 70x7...

• "You have to forgive so that you can be free to live each day with peace in your heart. Let go of the hurts and pains and let God bring justice into your life." - Joel Olsteen

• "The weak can never forgive. Forgiveness is the attribute of the strong." - Mahatma Gandhi,
All Men Are Brothers: Autobiographical Reflections

• "People are often unreasonable and self-centered. Forgive them anyway. If you are kind, people may accuse you of ulterior motives. Be kind anyway. If you are honest, people may cheat you. Be honest anyway. If you find happiness, people may be jealous. Be happy anyway. The good you do today may be forgotten tomorrow. Do good anyway. Give the world the best you have and it may never be enough. Give your best anyway.

SIX FEET DEEP

For you see, in the end, it is between you and God. It was never between you and them anyway." - Mother Teresa

- "To be a Christian means to forgive the inexcusable because God has forgiven the inexcusable in you." - C.S. Lewis

- "True forgiveness is when you can say, thank you for that experience." - Oprah Winfrey

- "Forgiveness is not an occasional act, it is a constant attitude." - Martin Luther King, Jr.

- "People have to forgive people. We don't have to like them, we don't have to be friends with them, we don't have to send them hearts in text messages, but we have to forgive them, to overlook, to forget. Because if we don't we are tying rocks to our feet, too much for our wings to carry." - C. JoyBell C.

- Forgiven people forgive. Bitter on your part, is litter in your heart.
- When you forgive those who have hurt you - you free yourself! Nothing is worth derailing your destiny!

- Being "right" often costs us being loved. Release all that is not love from your heart, and simply forgive.

- 1 cross + 3 nails = 4 given

- Freely forgive and live freely

- When someone hurts you, you don't have to hurt back. God is your vindicator!

Chapter 19
Choices

Every day we make choices and those choices determine our destiny. Some choices are good while others can be costly. We often blame others for the results that we face such as: growing up on the wrong side of town, one or both parents were alcoholics or addicted to drugs, addiction to gambling, or we were lured by someone else's influence which caused us to make those wrong choices. We tend to blame others for our own miseries, as it's easier to say, "You are the one who made my life miserable." However in all actuality, no one can make our lives into anything. True they can inflict pain physically and verbally, and they can throw obstacles in your path, but they can't make your life anything unless you allow them to. Life is full of obstacles, storms, trials, difficulties, and injustices. It's almost a guarantee that these are going to happen, but here's the important question about them. How are you going to handle them? It doesn't matter who or what causes these confrontations. What does matter is how you respond to and deal with them. I once heard years ago, "How you respond to a situation within the first ten-seconds will determine the outcome." It only makes sense. If you immediately hand the matter over to the Lord, it's no longer yours to deal with. Granted you may need to also seek Him for guidance or strength in the matter, but and then you start offering Him the praises for His intervention. On the other hand, if you immediately start yelling, screaming, cursing, and handle the matter in a fleshly manner with hate, bitterness, and unforgiveness, don't blame anyone else except yourself when your turmoil doesn't improve. We do have the ability and the authority to say how this chapter in our life will end. It's our choice to either allow others to control us, or for us to control our own destiny.

The opening chapters in the Bible gave us an example of the first choices mankind was given to be able to make. It was the choice to eat or not to eat the fruit from the tree of knowledge. The choice Adam and Eve made, known as the Fall of Man, has effected all of mankind ever since.

Here are some interesting points about choices: First, there is no in between. There's no such thing as a half-truth or white lie; there's no such thing as drivng a car if you choose to leave the transmission in park; when it comes to voting it's either for or against a person or issue; when you flip the light switch it's either on or off. Decisions are made for one direction or another.

Forgiving someone is a choice…it's your choice. It all boils down to making your choice to do it God's way or your way. When you choose to forgive it fulfills God's Word and purpose and allows His blessings to fill your life. When you choose to not forgive it's the fulfillment of fleshly desires and reaps calamity. It matters to God how you treat others. "If anyone boasts, "I love God" and goes right on hating his brother or sister, thinking nothing of it, he is a liar. If he won't love the person he can see, how can he love the God he can't see? The command we have from Christ is blunt: Loving God includes loving people. You've got to love both." 1 John 4:20 (MSG)

- Never condemn another person for not forgiving someone if you yourself haven't forgiven someone else.

- "When you choose to forgive, you free yourself from being a prisoner to that other person and or the event. Nothing is worth missing your destiny - let it go and watch God work in your behalf."
  - Paula White

Choices

- "Choose forgiveness - it is not an emotion - it is a choice."

  - Cheryl Bramlett
  7 Steps to Finding Freedom
  Through The Power of Forgiveness

Offering forgiveness does not always lead to a healed relationship. Some people are not capable of love because of their own hidden hurts. It might be wise to let them go on to their own separate way. Wish them well and continue to pray for them.

The Lord has a mysterious and marvelous way of creating and replacing those old relationships with new ones. He will cause your paths to cross with others to help you along the bumpy and crooked roads to become one that is a smooth highway. One of His promises to you is, "The crooked places shall be made straight, and rough ways smooth; And all flesh shall see the salvation of the Lord." (Is. 40:4; Luke 3:5 NKJV)

Offering forgiveness does however, place you in the place of right standing with our Lord. Fulfilling His instructions, living with the manifested fruits of the Holy Spirit in your life, opens the pathway for His righteousness in you.

It's my prayer that you have searched and cleansed your heart from all unforgiveness. I pray that you have thrown away all the anger, strife, bitterness, jealousy, lies, and any sin which separates you from the Lord that you have harbored in your heart, and have replaced these areas with love and forgiveness.

CLOSING THOUGHTS

I didn't choose to be kidnapped...but it happened
I didn't choose to be physically abused...but it happened
I didn't choose to be sexually violated...but it happened
I didn't choose to be tied and bound in a bathroom...but it happened

SIX FEET DEEP

I didn't choose to live in children's and boys' homes...but it happened
I didn't choose to be lied to...but it happened
I didn't choose to be spit on...but it happened
I didn't choose to adopted...but it happened
I didn't choose to have my name changed...but it happened
I didn't choose to have my character slandered...but it happened
I did choose to forgive...and it happened.

Forgiveness is a choice...choose to forgive.

NOTES:

NOTES:

Enjoy these other titles from Bold Truth Publishing

The Replacement Theology LIE
by Adrienne Gottlieb

Effective Prison Ministries
by Wayne W. Sanders

FIVE SMOOTH STONES
by Aaron Jones

SPIRITUAL BIRTHING
Bringing God's Plans & Purposes and Manifestation
by Lynn Whitlock Jones

Lace, Lust & LIES
by Aaron Jones

KINGDOM of LIGHT II - kingdom of darkness
Spiritual Warfare and The Church
by Michael R. Hicks

The FAITH WALK
by Paul Howard

JOB'S JEOPARDY
by Barbara J. White

Seemed Good to THE HOLY GHOST
by Daryl P Holloman

VICTIM TO VICTOR
THE CHOICE IS YOURS
by Rachel V. Jeffries

Available now at Amazon.com

Check out all the Great Books from
BOLD TRUTH PUBLISHING